The Walk

The Walk

William deBuys

⬡ Trinity University Press
SAN ANTONIO

Published by Trinity University Press
San Antonio, Texas 78212

© 2007 by William deBuys

Cover design by Nicole Hayward
Typeset by BookMatters, Berkeley

♾ The paper used in this publication meets the minimum requirements of
the American National Standard for Information Sciences — Permanence
of Paper for Printed Library Materials, ANSI Z39.48-1992.

Library of Congress Cataloging-in-Publication Data
DeBuys, William Eno.
The walk / William deBuys.
p. cm.
  SUMMARY: "Set on the small farm in a New Mexico mountain valley
that the author has tended since 1976, the book explores how personal
history and natural history interweave in a familiar landscape. Three
interrelated essays move from conflict and loss in the author's life to a
place of acceptance" — *Provided by publisher.*
  ISBN 978-1-59534-027-6 (hardcover : alk. paper)
  1. Sangre de Cristo Mountains (Colo. and N.M.) — Description and
travel. 2. Sangre de Cristo Mountains (Colo. and N.M.) — Biography.
3. DeBuys, William Eno. 4. DeBuys, William Eno — Travel — Sangre
de Cristo Mountains (Colo. and N.M.) 5. Natural history — Sangre de
Cristo Mountains (Colo. and N.M.) 6. Landscape — Sangre de Cristo
Mountains (Colo. and N.M.) 7. DeBuys, William Eno — Homes and
haunts — Sangre de Cristo Mountains (Colo. and N.M.) 8. Farm life —
Sangre de Cristo Mountains (Colo. and N.M.) 9. Mountain life —
Sangre de Cristo Mountains (Colo. and N.M.) 10. Sangre de Cristo
Mountains (Colo. and N.M.) — Social life and customs. I. Title.
F802.S35D445 2007
917.88'49—dc22   2007003212

17 16 15 14 13 12 — 5 4 3 2

for Alex, Margaret, Will, and Eliza

Contents

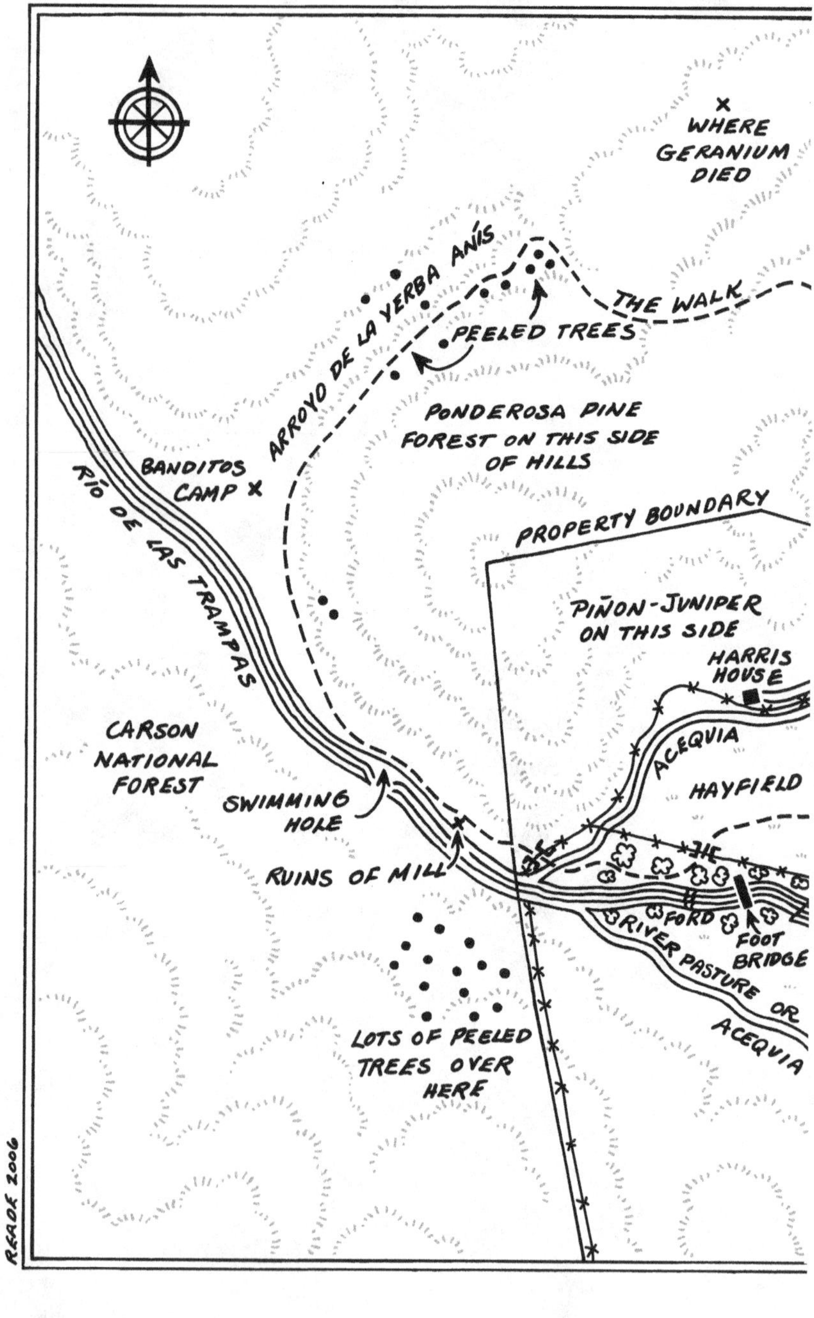
WHERE GERANIUM DIED
ARROYO DE LA YERBA ANÍS
THE WALK
PEELED TREES
PONDEROSA PINE FOREST ON THIS SIDE OF HILLS
BANDITOS CAMP
RÍO DE LAS TRAMPAS
PROPERTY BOUNDARY
PIÑON-JUNIPER ON THIS SIDE
HARRIS HOUSE
ACEQUIA
HAYFIELD
CARSON NATIONAL FOREST
SWIMMING HOLE
RUINS OF MILL
FORD
FOOT BRIDGE
RIVER PASTURE OR
ACEQUIA
LOTS OF PEELED TREES OVER HERE
READE 2006

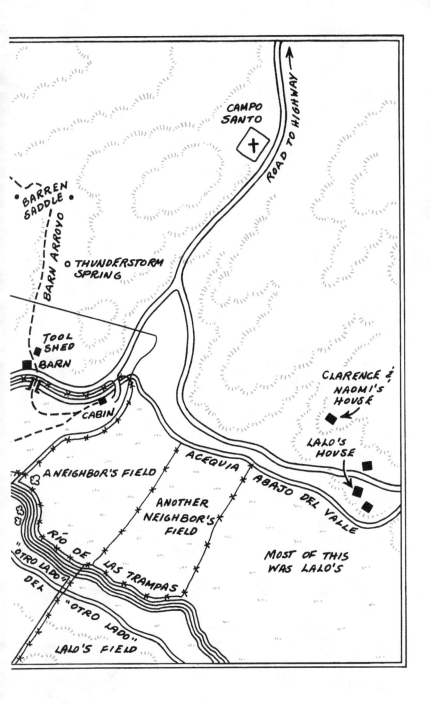

The Walk

A SPECIES OF HOPE resides in the possibility of seeing one thing, one phenomenon or essence, so clearly and fully that the light of its understanding illuminates the rest of life. Almost any object of contemplation can be the vehicle for such discovery. When I study the surface of the pine desk where I am writing and admire the faint green tint of the stain that penetrates the wood and the lines of darker grain that resist the stain, it takes no leap of imagination to reflect that each line of grain marks a year of growth and to be reminded that this wood was once the flesh of a living tree. Perhaps it stood within a forest on a western mountainside, one resembling the forest that enfolds the valley where this desk occupies the corner of a cabin, a forest that clothed itself in a green of which the stain of the desk is the merest echo, a forest that answered the wind with its own individual sound, singing or groaning when the wind tore through it. It would have been a forest that bore up to the lashing of rain, snow, and sun and that flourished under their mercies. It would have been a forest that harbored uncountable creatures from bacteria to bears, a biota always in tension, always dynamic, a living community of interrelations more complex than the most brilliant among us has the power to conceive. In this way, the grain of this pine desk becomes a portal to the complexity of creation.

Or I might dwell upon the view from the window above the desk. I have surely given hours enough, cumulative days, weeks, perhaps months of my life, to indolent gazing through these panes. Particularly in recent months I have contributed to that total with unprecedented, if reluctant, generosity as I have struggled to accept my newly single condition and the feeling of solitude that, uninvited, has become my closest companion.

I can describe for you with eyes closed the toolshed appended to the cabin and the crude ramada just beyond it that shelters a fire pit, dishwashing sink, and other elements of an outdoor kitchen. A little to the side, beneath the presently leafless branches of a tall, thick-trunked cottonwood, is the rust-colored but not rusting metal table where I eat when the weather allows, and beyond that the near fence with its sagging wires and canted juniper posts, and then the scruffy, tussocked hayfield, its pale stubble now yielding to a hint of green as the grasses awaken from winter's sleep. A stately line of Rocky

Mountain junipers — the closest thing we have to cedars, and so we also call them that — rims the field on the uphill side. The cedars mark the path of the irrigation ditch by which the field is nourished and made to grow a mix of grasses and legumes that comprise an excellent horse hay: alfalfa, clover, timothy, orchard grass, and smooth brome.

Without irrigation these plants would wither in the rainless early weeks of the growing season. With it, and with the help of neighbors, my absent partners in the land and I cut a yard-high bounty in late July or August, and although at our altitude we cut only once, we keep irrigating the stubble afterward to grow more grass for fall grazing. Behind the cedars and the irrigation ditch rise steep hills stippled with a scrub of one-seed junipers and gnarled pines. The trees grow widely spaced, and between them you see through to the pink ground, which is all but bereft of soil. Even at a distance, the fleshlike color of the land belies its aridity, for it is armored with gravels decayed from the red granites that underlie these stingy hills.

Beyond and above the hills spreads the blue and empty sky of New Mexico, the words of which name enchant me beyond reason, suggesting not only a particular home and geography but an existence and a history shared with others, a notion of belonging in time and place, the essence of community. I believe it was Willa Cather who said — and I quote approximately — that elsewhere the land has the sky as its ceiling, but here in New Mexico the sky has the land for its floor. Another writer, Ross Calvin, captured the essence of the matter in the title of his book *Sky Determines*. It is a sky that has shaped land and people not by what it gives but by what it does not have and therefore must withhold: water. Lacking a haze of moisture, it is a giant, deep, and expansive sky, a sky so thin and light that distant objects — the far horizon of blue mountains, a high-flying jet, or cranes passing overhead — seem nearer than they are. It is a sky so weightless and pure that one is tempted to believe it places no burden on the heads and minds beneath it, a sky under which it seems possible that thoughts might come more freely and less constrained than in other places. It is a sky of double lightness, of both illumination and weightlessness.

At no time do you sense this more than on a moonless night, gazing from this very window, or better, stepping onto the shallow porch of this two-room, mud-brick cabin to see the stars. We are far from the upwelling lights of any city. We are in a crescent-shaped valley cupped in the side of the Sangre de Cristo Mountains, well out of sight of the winding back road that connects Santa Fe and Taos. At night the blackness of our sky is truly black, the stars stunningly bright. Across the center of the heavens the Milky Way spreads like a smear of butterfat, shining so intensely that there seems to be no dark between the stars. It is a display so striking that one never tires of fetching binoculars and confirming with the aid of magnification that no matter where one looks, one sees light beyond light beyond light, stretching to infinity. And yet it is not infinity; it is only the Milky Way, our home galaxy. It seems to stretch to the limits of the universe, and yet we are in it. It is the embodiment of *out there*, and yet it includes us. In this way, the view from this cabin and its writing desk has the power to draw one's imagination to the limits of the cosmos.

Have no doubt, though — this cabin does not stand in Eden. The woodstove is smoking unpleasantly, and legions of spring flies that hatch in the pasture soil are on the march, buzzing toward the warmth of these adobe walls, creeping under the door sill or in through the walls, perhaps following the grain-wise splits in the roof beams, the round, whole logs we call vigas. Others penetrate gaps around the window moldings or through cracks I can neither fathom nor find. Only a few have yet arrived, for it is still early in April, but I know they are on their way, and their ranks will soon swell to become an army of distraction, of disturbance, of disgust. As even Eden had its snake, every cabin has its flies, and this one has more than any other I have known. There have been times, following long absences, when I have returned to find gruesome swarms of thousands of flies, alive, dead, and writhing in transition from one state to the other, blackening the window sills, corpses spilling to the floor. I tiptoe in, trying vainly not to step on any. From a corner of the room I retrieve a small vacuum cleaner that stands always at the ready. At the flip of a switch, the whine of its motor drowns out the seething buzz, and as clouds of flies vanish down the throat of the machine, the room fills with a cloying, sweet odor faintly redolent of peanut butter, which is the smell of fly bodies rendered by the violence of the vacuum into a mildly greasy dust.

Even when conditions are not so Hitchcockian, when only one or two fat survivors drone in circles through the rooms, the flies have an unsettling effect. They connect me to a history of two and a half decades of battling insects, mice, squirrels, wood rats, and other creatures that have vied to share this home with me and my now fractured family. The invasions have ranged from the vexing to the horrific. They tie me to my own, lamentably overdeveloped, capacity for impatience and frustration, and if I wanted to follow that thread still further, which I do not, I might easily tie it to every fault in my psychology, every episode of shortness, cruelty, petulance, self-pity — the list of possibilities might soon exhaust the most patient reader — of which I have been guilty. I digress in this manner only to make the point that almost any stimulus — the taste of a madeleine or the buzzing of a fly — may lead anywhere, including inward by way of faults, feelings, or details of personal history to take us on an inner journey of unlimited extent.

The study of character — our own or others' — is really the study of the world, for all that we keep of the world we capture in our memories and feelings, which feed the formation of character. The most powerful of those memories connect to the deaths and losses, the departures of love, the realizations of imperfection and unrequitedness that have both opened and broken our hearts. Ultimately these feelings bring us back to the unavoidable solitude of the self, where we ponder how to live and be, how to transcend or make peace with the aloneness of consciousness. And where we also ponder how we might find in our existential solitude the link to solidarity and fellowship and even to intimacy with the soul of another. In this way, we can travel great distances on the back of a buzzing fly.

But these journeys, however small their point of origin and infinite their possibility, exist only in the mind, and as living creatures you and I are but half comprised of mind. Our other half is corporeal, and a body wants to move. So taking hat and coat on a breezy day, we go out. We walk.

The walk I would take you on is one I have been making for twenty-seven years. A dispassionate observer, watching from afar, might say that for more than a quarter century I have been going in circles, round and round the same hill. Sometimes with family or friends, more often alone, in all seasons and weathers, all times of day and even night, rain and snow, sun and moon, around I go, up one arroyo, down another, back by the river and the ancient mill, and up through the farm. Or clockwise, the other way around. I may even have made the circuit a time or two in my dreams, for there are places I feel sure I have visited—a coyote den in an arroyo bank, a bear trail up high on the canyon side—and to which I have tried to return, but the places seem to have disappeared. I concede that perhaps they never existed. I am twenty-seven years invested in making this circuit, in mulling and trying to read the story of a single landscape over a long time, in using the same walking meditation to hear, or at times quiet, the voices inside my head. The walk is like a piece of music that I partly play and partly listen to, a theme-and-variation composition built up from hundreds of rehearsals and excursions. Having now spent slightly more than half my life studying this score, I feel I am still trying to learn it, still trying to understand my part and how to play it.

I do not always take the walk on foot. Many are the times I have ridden it, or parts of it, on the back of a horse. It is not hard to summon up twenty-seven years of mounts: King, Prince, Flo, Geranium, Spottie, Babe, Dandy, Sundown, and Smokey. Any of them, even with caution in the canyon rocks, could have made the loop in fifteen minutes without being much winded at the end. On foot it's a forty-minute stroll, if you take the route that's most direct, which I rarely do. I am a slower version of the three generations of border collie that have kept me company on these rounds: Creeper, Ike and Sadie, Wes. The dogs trot the trail, then catch a scent and veer into the brush. It's the same, in a way, for me. I walk or ride a horse, thinking I am going straight along, but then a sound, a glint of light, a stray idea—some tug on sense or mind—and I see I am headed somewhere else: to the boneyard where I shot the mare, to a check dam in the arroyo, to a well-known tree or rocky outcrop, or to no certain place at all. I take the walk, and then the walk takes me.

The pace of choice for venturing into the woods, according to the most celebrated of American walkers, is the saunter. Henry David Thoreau boasted that he sauntered daily and for hours through the Concord woods, and he relished the derivation of the word. It originated, he said, nearly a thousand years ago, in the time of the Crusades, when Europe swarmed with pilgrims bound for the Holy Land, "*à la Sainte Terre*." Not every pilgrim marched with resolution nor meant to reach Jerusalem. Indeed, not every pilgrim was a pilgrim, for many used the spirit of their time as a cover for self-indulgent travel, unstructured rambling, and directionless exploring. Respectable people disparaged these half-hearted pilgrims as *Sante-Terrers* — saunterers. Such was the judgment of purposeful burghers, but not of Henry Thoreau. On no class of human being does he lavish higher praise than on the saunterers of Europe as it awakened from the Dark Ages. In the freedom with which they wandered and in their presumed openness to exploration and discovery, Thoreau found both metaphor and precedent for the way he wished to live.

To saunter is to exercise the first of all freedoms, which is mobility, and to do so well one must go out with a mind as unfettered as the body. One goes forth limber in every aspect, legs swinging easily, arms loose and free. One's eyes are alive to color, pattern, and movement, one's ears alert to birdcall and wind song. The nose and tongue are gladdened by the taste of the day, and the chest fills not just with good rich air but also with exultation, or at least a sense of its possibility. The world seems open and generous, and the mind enters it, wandering as freely as the feet. Often a kind of marvelous mystery then unfolds, which no one can explain. It is the mystery of how walking lubricates the connections of thought, loosens the bonds on the subconscious, and allows unknown and unexpected ideas and feelings to surface—often the very idea or feeling or insight we have been seeking for weeks. It is the mystery of how walking helps the mind go out and the world come in, and brings us to our senses.

At least that is how a good saunter is supposed to work, and for me it sometimes does, but I cannot always match Henry Thoreau's cocky, not-a-care-in-the-world attitude. Sometimes I don't saunter so much as I plod or even trudge, weighed down with cares and disappointments. In fairness, I suspect Henry had his heavy-footed days too, and if he did, he no doubt learned that by the end of a good walk his step was often lighter than when he started out. Sometimes the easiest answer to our difficulties is not so much to get outside ourselves as simply to get ourselves outside. I find this especially true when I walk in deeply familiar territory.

On my twenty-seven-year circuit up and down arroyos and back by the river and the field, the layering of repetition and memory has so twined my sense of the land with my sense of my own past that one leads to the other and back again without the least interruption. I don't mean that every step along the way or every tree I pass evokes memory of a specific event, although some do. It is more like being present in a house where one has lived a long time. At one time or another, one has felt the full range of possible feelings in every room, and one has looked out each window in every possible state of mind and condition of weather. And the fact of all that history heavying the air and coating the walls somehow makes it easier to reenter the gamut of those feelings, and all the states of mind that go with them. It is as though one's awareness of place and awareness of self had grown together like two plants in the same pot, so that their enmeshed roots formed a single web of memory. And out of that web sprout stems and branches that are similarly entwined, so much so that the body of one plant cannot be distinguished, let alone separated, from the other, the parts of each leading to the parts of the other and affording quite surprising potential for connection, serendipity, and sudden discovery. In such a way, a homely well-worn path becomes a route into and through the self, leading to destinations unimagined. This is the paradox of the familiar: the more you know a place, or think you know it, the more it can take you where you do not expect.

So out we go, you and I, not really knowing where we are bound, and we saunter or, as the case may be, trudge along the scruffy upper edge of the hayfield, past the outhouse to the center gate, which we do not open. It is simpler to step atop the sawn side-stump of the big cedar that anchors the gate and steady ourselves by grasping the stub of a long-dead branch, as we swing first one leg and then the other over the barbed wire, stepping down onto the stump of another side-trunk and then to the ground. Every farm has such odd adaptations: a quirky stile to traverse a fence, a hidden bench where the shade is best, a hollow tree to hide a shovel. Such habits and structures make a landscape personal. The gesture may be as small as a coffee can for spare keys hidden at the foot of a tree or as large as a hay barn or a toolshed built to fit a certain site. We pass all of these things now as we take the trail that follows the trace of a wagon road up an arroyo and into the woods, and we are walking.

I call this the Barn Arroyo, although it may have had another name years ago, before I built the barn. It drains a small and not very steep watershed in the saddle between two hills, and it has always provided a convenient path out of the valley and into the forest that enfolds it. In days gone by when people produced less waste and the waste was less objection-able, the people who tended this land used the arroyo as a dump. A mass of rusted cans and other detritus spills down the eroded slope toward the arroyo bottom. You see among the cans the archeology of lost usefulness: the fractured steering wheel of a tractor, the wooden arm of a chair, a bent rifle bar-rel, patches of leather from a boot, the housing for an oil filter. For years I too have used the arroyo as a dump, but in a different way. Along the forty or fifty yards that I can drive my truck up the trail, I have cut openings in the wall of piñon and juniper lining the arroyo so that I can throw into the gully tree trimmings, rotted fence posts, or willows cleared from the irri-gation ditch. In one place, the accumulation of organic waste is yards deep, a dense, tangled mass representing years of detri-tus. On the rare occasions, seldom more than two or three a year, when heavy rains cause the arroyo to flow, the resulting flash floods now encounter such a wall of obstacles that, instead of eating the channel deeper, they slow and release their load of silt. Storm by storm, they bury the branches and stems I fling in their path, and the bed of the arroyo rises. In a few places, grasses and mountain mahogany have taken root in the new, fine-grained deposits, and the gash of the arroyo is covering itself little by little with a living skin. There are other gashes and imperfections along this trail. Some are obvious, some hidden. Some are healing; some are not. The landscape abounds with flaws, like those who walk it.

It is good to see that a kind of healing is also taking place in the lumpy April soil of the trail. Winter's freezing and thawing have pushed up the surface of the ground in ropy, clay-bound chunks, as though it were stamped like a tin ceiling. The effect is equivalent to cultivation, aerating the soil and opening it to the penetration and germination of seeds. It also leaves it in a condition that records the track of every well-weighted foot that falls on it. The passage of a mouse may no more than blur the dirt, but here I see my boot print from a walk on another day, and there is the track of my dog. More interesting are the tracks of the larger wildlife, especially coyote, elk, and turkey, all of which are recorded in the traffic of the trail.

Coyotes have been common here seemingly forever. From my first days in this valley, their mad songs have been a particular joy of early summer. It may be as late as June when the year's pups leave the dens where they were whelped and begin to rove with the rest of the pack through the half-light of dawn and dusk. They soon join the adults in serenade, or try to, and the result can be bizarre. The pups haven't yet learned to sing. Their voices crack; they fail to hold the pitch or complete the phrase; they moan and hoot, sounding like tomcats or owls. Their inexperience briefly fills the valley with a spirit of comedy. You stop and smile. You wonder if the ravens are amused, or if the slow-witted gophers peer dimly from their burrows wondering if their oppressors are finally dying or insane. The episode passes in a moment, but a spirit of absurdity hangs in the air as the echoes of the botched concert fade. You realize that even the orchestra of nature needs tuning once in a while. And gradually the tuning is achieved. The incompetence of the coyote pups lasts only an outing or two. Soon they get the hang of singing like the big dogs so that the daily yipping and yowling that echoes through the valley reacquires its practiced character and again embodies, as perfectly as any sound on earth, a rhapsody of wildness.

The real news about wildlife here concerns the elk and turkey. Twenty-seven years ago, elk might be found only in the high country, the snowcapped heights of which I see looking eastward from the farm. The peaks form a majestic horizon. The river that nourishes this valley and its village is born in the seeps beneath the snowfields of the peaks and in the lakes and bogs at their feet. My farm lies fourteen miles downstream of those headwaters, at the bottom of our crescent valley, at an elevation of just under eight thousand feet. Some of the peaks jut a mile higher into the sky, topping thirteen thousand feet. The intervening distance leaves room for our ragged village of fifty or sixty souls to sprawl upstream from my place for a couple of valley miles, and then for a lot of rugged and wintry country to swell in long ridges from the village to the peaks. In all that distance, there are no other settlements — only a seldom-used cabin or two and one or two notable pioneering families hardy enough to live snowbound through the worst of the winter. It is wild country, which grows wilder past the rocky horizon of the high peaks, where the inner fastness of the Pecos Wilderness unfolds a land of rocky trails and rockier streams, spruce forests and constant wind. Years ago one encountered elk only up there. Even in winter when snow forced the herds to lower elevations, they didn't come this way. They went to distant winter grounds to the south and east.

With time the herds grew, and elk spilled this way, first only in harsh winters, later as a nearly year-round presence. And their numbers still grow. I remember on a ride a dozen years ago coming upon a cluster of strangely mangled yuccas of the variety fancifully called Spanish bayonet. The bayonet part is apt, for each of the stiff, fibrous leaves that cluster from the roots ends in a dark, vegetal stiletto. Were you unlucky enough to be thrown from your horse onto such a landing place, you would be a mass of lacerations when you limped away, if you got away at all. So it was surprising to come across a scattering of yuccas with their defenses overcome. Something had trampled down the dagger leaves and eaten out the juicy hearts.

Our neighborhood had a new presence. It was months before I realized the newcomers were elk, which have since prospered to such a degree that nowadays in our hills, yuccas are rarer than the elk used to be.

Turkeys, too, have become common, and thank goodness. It is always a pleasure, and not a rare one, to see them grazing at the end of the hayfield in midwinter. At first you think you see a copse of feathery gray bushes — except one or two bushes, and then all of them, may be seen to move, slowly stalking across the half-frozen ground, hunting grubs and pecking at sprigs of grass. Turkeys are as wary as any creature in the woods, and soon they sense they are being observed. When they flush, they labor upward, fat round wings beating the air. They fly slowly and awkwardly, gliding at the first chance, as though flight were a burden they were glad to put down. You watch them go, and you are sure you will get another look at them because you saw exactly where they went and they are so improbably big and ungainly that they are sure to be conspicuous. You saw thirty of them fade into three or four trees at the edge of the woods.

You train the binoculars on a pine where at least seven lighted. But there are no big lumps on the branches. Nothing. How can that be? You scan the hillside. Still nothing. No movement. Not even the tremble of a branch. The turkeys have melted away. Sly and stealthy, they are avatars of hidden grace and intelligence.

Turkeys nearly vanished from these hills in the 1950s. DDT,

more than anything, did them in. In the late forties and fifties, the Forest Service resolved to apply to forestry the same organizational skills and the same devotion to technology and logistics that the men then leading it had learned in defeating Germany and Japan. And they had a new tool to use, a miracle chemical that would kill bark beetles and budworms, the insect pests that preyed upon the trees that they thought would better serve society if converted into lumber. The Forest Service embarked on a program of aerial spraying that rained DDT upon the forests of northern New Mexico the way phosphorous bombs had previously rained on Dresden and Tokyo. Never mind that no one seriously thought about the effects of the pesticide on creatures other than insects. Nor that a majority of the people in the mountains then relied for drinking and cooking water on the irrigation ditches that ran by every house, ditches that were fed by the mountain streams into which the DDT inevitably washed.

It is chilling to imagine the technological hubris that infected the Forest Service. The agency sprayed the mountain forests liberally, repeatedly, and for all intents and purposes indiscriminately. Vast expanses were sprayed multiple times in a single year, not in order to achieve a specific biological effect but to meet delivery targets: so many tons of chemical applied to an impressive number of acres — if you spray them twice, you count them twice and boost your numbers. The idea was to apply your unit's full allocation of chemical. Where and how the poison was dumped was less important than the fact of dumping it: what mattered was to get it out of the airplane.

No one, to my knowledge, has assessed the effect of broad-scale DDT applications on human health in northern New Mexico, but I remember how strange it seemed in the 1970s that many middle-aged women in the mountain villages were succumbing to cancer. And why women more than men? In the years of heavy spraying, most of the village men and many of its male teenagers left the mountains for all but the winter months to earn cash wages elsewhere as herders, miners, and fieldworkers. Their exposure to summer spraying was less than that of the women. Or so it has seemed to me. I have no data, only the impression of too many women dying too young.

The effect on wild turkey, however, was clear. Like eagles, ospreys, and other creatures high on the food chain, they absorbed the concentrations already amassed by their prey, mostly canopy bugs and the crawlies of the forest duff. Poisoned by DDT, they laid eggs with shells too weak to bear the stress of delivery and incubation, and their chicks died unhatched.

In our area their numbers did not rebound until the 1980s, when giant, trident-shaped claw prints again began to appear in the mud of snowmelt and thunderstorm, as they appear now along the trail of the Barn Arroyo. The tracks lead everywhere. They tell a story of milling and foraging, as fifteen or even twenty birds drifted up the narrow drainage. The recovery of this big, odd, improbable creature came about thanks to the hard-won cessation of a grievous stupidity. It testifies to the resilience of the land. Even so, the recovery took a quarter of a century.

From my vantage, now past fifty, a quarter century seems a meaningful span. I was twenty-five when I came to this valley. A year and a half later, I began to irrigate the hayfield where this walk begins, and I have kept irrigating it ever since. The ruins of a gristmill may be found in the river canyon just downstream of my land — this walk will lead us there. Tree-ring analysis places the cutting date for one of its palings at 1816, the probable year the mill was built. This suggests that my hayfield has been irrigated at least since then and perhaps for several decades longer. When I do the math, I am surprised to realize that my share of that history is consequential. For at least a tenth of the years that farmers have nurtured my field by irrigation, I have been the farmer. These days, I wonder less than I used to whether I belong here. And I have no plans to go away. If fortune smiles and my health holds, I'll irrigate this field a quarter century more.

I have reached the low, nearly barren saddle that divides the Barn Arroyo from the larger watershed of *el arroyo de la yerba anís*. Archeologists would call this a deflated site, the deflation being the work of sheet erosion and wind scour to peel back the surface of the site, removing the small amounts of organic matter that accumulated when the land was healthier, and then working down through the naked clays. Such sites are good for finding the things that erosion leaves behind, and indeed many years ago my then-wife, Anne, found an obsidian arrowhead here. It lay fully exposed on the bare ground, uncovered by a recent storm. Its edges were perfect, the tip still sharp enough to cut or penetrate. Whether it had belonged to Pueblo or Apache is hard to say, and either is equally likely. Picurís Pueblo is only a few miles to the north, and bands of Jicarilla Apaches roamed these hills for generations. The small black point might also have belonged to a Hispano settler or a Comanche drawn from the plains to the settlements to raid or trade. Either might have used the weapons of the other, for in their distant day anything that served for fighting or hunting was good enough to buy, swap, or steal. Perhaps that's one reason we don't find arrowheads often here, for in the days when they were used, the loss of a single arrow was a palpable decline in wealth.

This land is generous with its beauty but not with the means of living. Its winters and droughts are too long, and its soils, outside the alluvium of the valley bottoms, too thin to yield more than a spare existence. The people who have eked out subsistence from these hills have been as tough and enduring as the piñon and juniper that border this all-but-barren site. None of the trees tops fifteen feet, and every one is spiny with dead branches, shaggy with the tendrils of lichens, gnarled and knotty. Yet the wood is dense and aromatic, and it burns with a steady flame.

Similar woodlands clothe the slopes ringing the valley on the north, but the clothing is scanty. South-facing and sun-afflicted, with more bare soil than canopy, the woodlands appear half-dressed, but they conceal much. People call them fragile, a term that gets used too freely across the Southwest, as though to say it were the land's fault that it comes unglued under the assault of truck tires, munching herds, and armies of "users." But seen another way, the land is a marvel of tenacity. Its adaptations to aridity, fire, sun, and cold make it anything but fragile. The surprises that hide without shelter in this stripped-down environment have always seemed to me more stunning than those that lurk in wetter, taller woods. One finds here the claret cup cactus that exults in red blossoms even before the rest of the land fully wakes from winter. It is here that nighthawks sleep on the ground during the day, only to explode into flight beneath your horse's hooves. And it is here that the weirdest and most unexplainable things occur when extremes of weather punish the land.

Once, riding home in a drenching thunderstorm through the saddle between watersheds at the head of Barn Arroyo, I saw a feature of the land I never dreamed possible. My horse Dandy, a young and jumpy black Arab, was winded. We'd tried to race the storm and get to shelter before it broke, but we lost the race. I had brought no slicker, and both of us were as drenched as if we had swum a river. Since we had nothing dry left to protect, there was no point in churning the arroyo trail or risking a slip in the greasy footing. We walked, as the rain poured. The mud sucked at Dandy's feet, and fat raindrops pelted us. They pocked the ground and made the branches of the trees dance. Their cumulative roar rang in our ears, punctuated by thunder. Dandy tried to shake the water from his head, but it was no use. The rain fell in sheets. Then I heard a new voice in the roar, a wet-sounding growl, and I looked for floodwater coursing down the arroyo. Nothing there. The sound came from higher up on the hill across the arroyo. I held Dandy back. The new growl grew louder. We eased down the slippery trail to get a fresh view through the trees.

There it was: halfway up the slope, a fountain of water gushing from the ground. A spring. A fat rope of brown water improbably surging out of the earth on the steep side of a nearly barren hill.

It made no sense to me. It seemed impossible that so much water could collect in the small area of the hilltop, drain immediately into the ground, and pipe its way under the slope to spew out with such volume and violence. Strange to tell, this sudden and temporary spring was erupting from the driest patch of ground the hill offered, and the hill was as dry as any for miles around. I watched the spring a while, as Dandy grew impatient. He tossed his head, sidestepping and spinning in little arcs as he fought the hackamore. He kicked up the mud, pushing and backing against the reins. I would have dismounted, but Dandy was too close to spooking and I might not have been able to get back on him. At last, I gave the horse some rein, and we slogged homeward down the trail. The growl of the fountain receded into the roar of the storm, but its image remained. I still see it: water leaping from barren clay.

On reflection, as I write this, I realize that this essay is one of those unexpected, storm-borne things, and the storm that produced it is still blowing within me.

Crossing from the saddle at the head of Barn Arroyo, I enter the shade of tall, orange-barked ponderosa pines; I leave a last boot print on the naked soil of the hard-used valley and step into the forest quiet, feeling the cushion of pine duff underfoot and smelling the tart decay of needles, bark, and wood. Everything changes: the quality of light, which now filters through the canopies of the big trees; the taste of the air; and the shape and content of what can be seen, for now the view in every direction is walled by the straight columns of tree trunks and roofed by high branches and boughs of slender green needles. All horizons have departed; no longer do the peaks loom in the southeast, nor is a visitor sensible of the encircling ridges. Even the sky is unavailable; I am entirely contained by the forest. Yet the containment is large and expansive; its limits move as I move, and it soothes with a particular stillness. For the moment there is no wind, and the silence of the forest is as soft as pine straw.

Henry Thoreau might saunter through this changed world, but something slows me down. The shadows of the forest invite a change of pace; sometimes they insist on it. Several paths diverge at the entry to the forest. I might take the trail to the knoll where the skull and spine of the aged mare still lie, only yards from where I shot her. Or I might head for the winterfat meadow, split by Arroyo Yerba Anís, where elk tracks dimple the soil. Or I might take the trail I cut myself, which winds to a point farther down the arroyo before bending, like all the other routes, toward the river. I take the last of these.

I do not go far before I stop. No matter the route, I must stop. Perhaps a breeze stirs, and a murmur drifts down from the foliage of the treetops. Perhaps the breeze becomes a wind, and the whisper of the boughs grows into a steady plaint. It is a curious thing, but every forest sings in its own distinctive key, and here, no matter whether the song murmurs, keens, or howls, the forest speaks in a dialect peculiar to these embattled ponderosas and the lesser trees that crowd their shadows. The first whisper of it bids me listen.

In extolling the saunter, the cocky Mr. Thoreau told only part of the story. We walk to wander, but we also walk to stop — and to wonder. The classical poets knew this. *Siste viator!* they commanded. "Pause, traveler." Virgil and his compeers wrote of moments when the journeying hero stopped or was compelled to stop by unknown powers and suddenly became privileged to glimpse beyond the boundaries of the mortal world. In such a moment Aeneas might behold a god or recognize the shades of the dead, and poets like Virgil made those moments central to their narratives.

The moment of encounter might occur anywhere — at a shrine, a grave, a crossroads, or at a place of no evident distinction. The moment itself was the important thing, for in its brief span it allowed the interpenetration of this world with the world of the spirit. It was also a moment of peril, for although the hero gladly surrendered to benign forces, he might as easily find himself confronted by a demon.

We nonheroes may not risk possession by demons or deities, but few among us are so obdurate, especially in the shadowy grace of a forest, that we do not admit the possibility of revelation. Entering the depths of a forest, we feel a shift in the mood of the land; the sound of the wind, of the stillness, of our own footsteps comes to us in a new language. Perhaps a display of beauty unfolds before us — snow falling like jewels through dawn light. Perhaps an owl hoots or a hermit thrush pipes its lament in a way that opens us to the uncommon, so that something within us releases. To stop and consciously open one's senses in the course of a walk is to pose a kind of question, which may or may not receive an answer. And when a reply appears, whether manifesting in the landscape or welling up from within, it may be so partial or inscrutable that it may seem to count for nothing. The solidity of the answer, however, is not the point. The point lies in making oneself available to the numinous, opening to see what comes. One time in twenty, or a hundred, or a thousand, something does. Every walk and every landscape carries the potential for unexpected revelation, and so, *siste viator*, one stops, looks, and listens. And what comes, comes.

For twenty-seven years, what comes first after I cross from the Barn Arroyo saddle and stop among the ponderosas is the joy of forest vision. How can I explain it? A pleasure so sensual will not submit to words. It has to do with the mottling of light and shadow on the infinitely varied trunks, which are themselves mottled in orange and black and in an infinite range of textures, most of them coarse, but some as smooth as river stones, as where lightning or some other force has peeled the bark away, leaving the inner wood to shine like a yellow beacon. The result delights the eye with no end of pattern and variation. Pleasure resides even more in the depth of the view, which accumulates, trunk by trunk, into a kind of visual palisade, but a palisade with no fixed location. It is a wall of containment that floats in the near distance yet recedes as far as sight can travel. It moves with you in any direction, as though you wore it like a giant hoopskirt. It is penetrable yet absolute; there is no seeing past it. The night sky embodies a similar unboundedness in its endless repetition of stars. In the forest, the heavens' sensation of infinity comes all the way down to earth.

My feeling for the forest has changed much in the years I have known it. The shift in feeling derives partly from what I have learned about the woods and partly from changes I have observed in the woods themselves. These are easy to see once you know what to look for. My first twenty years in this place coincided with one of the wettest periods in the reconstructed climate history of the Southwest. It was a good time to be a seed, then a seedling, then a sapling. The understories of ponderosa forests, which at the beginning of the period were already dense with growth, thickened into jungles of thin stems. The change was slow and gradual but impossible to miss: I stopped riding as randomly as I once had, as more and more the thickets of new growth compelled me to stick to trails and logging roads.

Abruptly the weather's generosity stopped. Beginning late in 1995, years of drought began to alternate with years of marginal sufficiency, and the jungle sickened. Some of the upstart trees perished and now stand dry and brittle, torches awaiting the flame. Others survived but barely, and now, much like the sun-blasted dwarf trees of the Barn Arroyo, they bristle with dead twigs and branches, and tassels of mosslike lichens dangle from their withered branches. This beleaguered generation is an ecumenical group. Piñon, juniper, Douglas fir, white fir, and countless young ponderosas find their place within it, but the net effect is everywhere the same: more trees crowd the forest floor than available water can support, and thus the young strangle each other as they also slowly strangle the big trees towering over them. These mature, thick-barked ponderosas, which by good fortune survived successive onslaughts of logging, now face an equal threat, which comes in two forms: death by desiccation (in which the ultimate executioner may be insects or disease) and death by fire.

The short history of the origin of this lamentable state of affairs is a story much like that of DDT. It is a story of hubris, misapplied technology, and a kind of managerial fundamentalism that insisted blindly that nature was as simple as the minds of those beholding it. The story said that fire injured the forest when in fact it maintained the forest's health. The prophecy, however, was self-fulfilling. Banishing fire led to conditions in which fire must return as a destructive rather than renewing force.

By burning through the grasses of the forest floor, the fires of ages past cleaned the forest of clutter, limiting the accumulation of fuels and killing the seedlings of trees that might have competed with the old-growth giants for space and water. But heavy grazing removed the fuels that carried such fires, and on its heels came the doctrine of total fire suppression. Where the doctrine most failed was in assuming that fire might be forever banished. It was an assumption that defied logic, and experience has since mocked it scornfully. Fuel accumulates. Dry, hot weather returns. Lightning or a knucklehead with a match provides a spark. Things burn. The greater the accumulation of fuel, the hotter the fire. The hotter the fire and the taller the cluttered fuels of the forest understory, the more the grand old trees are endangered. Fire climbs the vegetation of the understory like a ladder: from resin-rich duff to the ground-sweeping branches of a juniper and up through the juniper and into the scrawny Douglas fir or pine leaning over it, and up through the top branches of that tree, leaping skyward, finally to ignite the canopy of the regal ponderosas. The result is a crown fire, with flames racing fatally from the top of one tree to the next.

In a ponderosa pine forest, if fire is denied expression in relatively frequent, low-intensity events, it will collect its due ultimately in massive, apocalyptic ones. Sooner or later in the dry woody corners of an oxygen planet, things burn.

But those concerns entangle us in the future. What does one say to the present moment and its paradox? Here I stand in a forest riven with illness, out of balance, disordered, a place of problems. Yet it is undeniably a delight to the senses. It gives pleasure, eliciting affection. The caress it offers may be the touch of the misshapen hand, but the caress is no less delicate, sensuous, and welcome. The forest asks us to love what is marred. It shows us the scarred face of beauty, the smile of broken teeth.

Perfection, in a way, is simple. Things that are unblemished — Keats's urn, the heartthrob's face — have a simplicity and coherence that seem radiant, transcendent. Age and time have not affected them. Their elegance shimmers, seemingly immortal. But add a crack to the Grecian urn or crow's-feet around the eyes of Venus or Adonis, and history and complexity intrude. We cannot ignore that something has happened. Something is continuing to happen. And in this world beyond the gates of Eden, if time passes and things keep happening, eventually suffering must intrude; it cannot be otherwise. And when suffering intrudes, still more complexity arises because suffering complicates our response to the world. We can ignore it. We can shut it out or at least try to. Or we can let it in so that we see it, hear it, and feel it, in which case our hearts begin to ache. And when our hearts ache, whether for the refugee, the absent lover, the sick friend, or the ailing forest, we feel them more, and they open wider.

Suddenly we are immersed in an ecology of compassion. The wide and open heart gives more love; the blemished, imperfect thing needs more love. One thing gives; the other receives; both benefit. Such is the species of justice that can arise in the overgrown forest, as it can also arise elsewhere. The forest through which we walk has been afflicted by time. It bears the scars of history and the wounds of fresh injury. This urn is a cracked and blemished vessel, and yet it brims with life.

Now a jay shrieks. A woodpecker drums. A chickadee sings its descending *dee, dee, dee, dee*. The music of nature is not less musical when it comes from a place of hardship. In this forest nature sings the blues, and the blues, rich with imperfection, can touch a soul as deeply as the music of the spheres.

I first came to this beautiful place of failure as a young man, never having failed at anything important, or rather not admitting to having done so. Real failure entails permanent loss, and at twenty-five or twenty-six years of age nothing in life seems permanent nor any loss irrevocable. At that age I believed every problem might be corrected, that love, passion, energy, and time might overcome all obstacles. Retrospectively such a belief seems as unfounded as the conviction that DDT might be benign, but at the time the world was new, unshadowed by the past and brimming with possibility.

In those days I spent a fair portion of my energy on forest affairs, especially the management of the forests around my village, arguing and working with the people of the Forest Service, some of whom I counted as friends. One practice I lobbied against was called precommercial thinning, in which crews chainsawed the piñon and juniper that encroached the pine stands and thinned the young ponderosas so that the remaining pines might grow fast and straight and arrive at the sawmill sooner. I argued against such market-driven efficiency, saying the juniper had as much right to populate the forest as the ponderosa. I knew nothing about the role of fire in forests or about the utility of thinning as a partial substitute for it, but I was rock-bottom certain I knew what was right.

Interestingly, the man we called the Timber Beast for our ranger district did not seem to know much about the ecology of the woods either. He mainly understood how to farm sawlogs and get them to market. He was an unhappy guy who lived alone and answered his door after dark with a semiautomatic in his hand. I never understood what he was afraid of. Certainly not me, although my periodic badgering may have contributed to his general air of discouragement. Which in turn may be a contributory reason for his abandonment of precommercial thinning. Far more likely, his program's budget shrank and left him without the means to pursue it. For whatever reason, the program came to a halt in the portion of the forest I possessively considered to be my concern. I regret that now. The thinning may have been merely palliative and its goals ill-conceived, but its effects tended in the right direction. Today when I visit places that were thinned under the program, they look better to me than places that weren't.

But while those mistakes of ecology and resource management are failures of importance, they exist in a world far beyond the limits of what I can expect to control. For errors scaled to my own life, I have the marriage I was then embarking on, helping to form. The marriage that began full of light and space and beauty, like a young forest. The marriage in which during those very years I was planting, together with my wife, the seeds of its ultimate undoing. I don't mean that I regret the marriage—far from it. I regret the way I coaxed those seedlings into saplings by means of habits and patterns I would have done better to burn away. But years pass, children are born, and life rolls by as the children grow and mature. The marriage, like a forest, thickens with the untended growth of busy years. And with children mostly grown, twenty-five or -six or -seven years later, suddenly there comes the drought, the dieback, and the big burn. In my case it crowned on the December solstice just past.

The winter that followed was a landscape of ashes and stumps, everything charred, and a deadening silence. That was the winter inside me. Externally the winter was merely mediocre, a season of meager snow and no bone-breaking cold. Just short, undramatic days, with no evident life in the land and the kind of chill that maintains a constant level of discomfort. I kept walking the walk, though. I walked it more often than ever. I kept circling the same hill through a forest with which I felt increasing kinship, a forest as imperfect and as mismanaged as I.

I did not saunter. I trudged, and often I trudged as a desperado, which is to say a man *des-esperado* — with hope removed. Millions go through divorce, and millions survive, but nearly all find themselves stripped to their essentials, wondering if their essentials are enough to get them through. I wondered plenty, and I did a lot of my wondering in the sick, beautiful forest of my twenty-seven-year walk. It became a kind of home when home was otherwise upended and dislocated. It also became the place to try to gather the pieces of my disassembled puzzle back together. I had started walking the walk in 1976, a year before Anne and I were married, and I have kept walking it weekly or at least monthly nearly every year thereafter. The pieces for which I searched had to be there somewhere. I kept looking. I kept looking in spite of the large gap, which the forest had a way of pointing out to me, between what I thought I was seeing and what was actually there. I kept looking in spite of frequent reminders of George Eliot's observation that "the quickest of us walk about well padded with stupidity."

By the late 1980s I had walked the walk for a dozen years. I knew every twist of trail. I knew the stumps and deadfalls as well as I knew the living trees. I knew where to cross the river when it swelled with snowmelt. I knew where to check for tracks of elk or turkey, to see if they were present and how they were behaving. I knew the old trails the first settlers had used and the vanishing traces of the wagon roads of horse-drawn days. I knew where the first spring flowers bloomed and which ravines the bears would rumble down to forage for acorns in the fall. I felt that the land was mine because I knew it and that I belonged to the land because it had told me so much of its story.

A retired forester called me up. Fred Swetnam had been a ranger on almost every district in northern New Mexico: Jemez, Canjilon, El Rito, Española, and Peñasco, which is now called Camino Real and includes the forests surrounding my farm. Years earlier I had interviewed Fred for a book I was writing. He had since retired to Española. We stayed in touch. He said he would like to visit, have a look at the woods, and discuss the condition of the forest. I said, Come on.

We spent a day walking old timber sales and bouncing down logging roads in Fred's truck. He spoke proudly of his sons, one of whom had distinguished himself as an ecologist and a leader in the field of dendrochronology, the study of tree rings. "Tom is even using tree rings to figure out the dates for peeled trees. Do you know what they are?" I had to confess I didn't. "The Indians, probably Apaches, would peel off the outer bark of the ponderosas to get at the cambium. They always peeled it more or less the same way, and they didn't girdle the tree, so it kept living—but with a visible scar. You can't miss seeing them."

We drove to a stand of ponderosas where Fred strode up to a large tree that bore the telltale scar. The peel was about four feet long and less than a foot wide, stretching from three feet off the ground to almost seven feet up the trunk, a comfortable height for a person of average build to work on the tree. It was very much at eye level. Hard to miss. But I had never noticed such a scar before.

Whoever removed the bark had effectively killed the area of the peel, which had remained a bare patch of weathered yellow wood for at least a century, possibly two. The vigor of the tree had not been affected. Its bushy green canopy soared seventy feet above us, as tall as any tree in the forest. "Over here," said Fred. He pointed to another tree with another peel. "And here." The one next to it also bore the scar of a peel, which regrowth had almost covered over. We were in a patch of forest only a few score yards from a trail I used frequently. An abandoned wagon road passed through the grove, and I had ridden along it at least a half dozen times, but I had never noticed the peels. Now I saw them on tree after tree. In only a few minutes Fred and I counted ten in the immediate area. Fred explained that the inner bark or cambium of the pines — the living tissue of the tree between the outer bark and the wood — had furnished a kind of food: the juices of the tree were rich in sugars. Trouble was, they were also rich in resins. Cutting the peel, so the story goes, was considered women's work; hence the old and unpleasant term *squaw tree*, which *peeled tree* has replaced. According to Fred, the details of how the bark was prepared to make it edible remained unclear. "They leached out the nasty stuff," he said, "or they only used it at a time of year when it wasn't so nasty. Either that or they had the digestive system of porcupines."

In time I learned more about peeled trees. I read a tale collected by the anthropologist Morris Opler in which Tanager teaches the Jicarilla Apache the use of various tree barks, including cottonwood and pine. He tells them to use a hard, pointed stub of oak or mountain mahogany to scrape away the outer bark and get to the edible flesh. Tanager tells them to do this in June when the inner bark is best to eat.

I also discovered the memoir of a forest ranger who served in the Pecos area in the 1920s and who heard the old-timers of his day explain how Apaches dried the pine cambium they collected and then ground it in a metate, making a kind of pine-bark flour that they mixed with other kinds of flour before eating. I got to know Fred Swetnam's son Tom, who for many years has headed the Laboratory of Tree-Ring Research at the University of Arizona in Tucson and whose analysis of successive fire scars on long-lived ponderosas and other tree species has done much to reconstruct the native fire frequency of southwestern forests. Using the same techniques, Tom has also dated peeled trees, determining the exact year when a given tree was peeled. In some locations he has found dozens of trees peeled in the same year — a phenomenon suggesting that pine bark might have served as a starvation food when nothing else was available. In other places, however, the dates of the peels are scattered over decades, possibly indicating that the food was used regularly but not intensively when people returned to an area.

The main idea that stayed with me after my day in the field with Fred Swetnam, however, had nothing to do with the cultural uses of pine bark. It was the realization that a remarkable and quite evident feature of the forest had escaped my notice for years. I had been blind when I thought I was observant. I had been dull when I thought I was sharp. It was as though my eyes had been clouded with cataracts, and for all the years I had explored the forest I had failed to see what was before me. Now those particular cataracts had been removed, and I began to notice peeled trees everywhere: in Cañada Corral and Cañada Orejón, places where I cantered my horses in long runs on soft ground; I found them on side slopes at the mouth of the cañoncito, where the river exited my pastures and plunged into a box canyon; I even found one near the barren saddle at the head of the Barn Arroyo, just a few paces off the trail. I found them nearly everywhere I looked, and I found them especially along the walk.

The trail I most often take descends from the Barn Arroyo saddle along a path I cut years ago, then picks up a seldom-used logging road that contours the slope, and follows it to a gully. From there a game trail leads down the gully through brush and big trees and out to the lower meadow of Arroyo Yerba Anís, which is a dry channel that flows only under the brunt of heavy storms. You step into the meadow through a gap between trees that is like a door. You emerge from the enclosure of the forest into the bright, unroofed openness of the meadow, and no matter how dark your mood, the sudden generosity of light and space jolts you with a pulse of joy. Here is an acre or more of low tawny grasses, blue grama and western wheatgrass, vigorous and mostly uncropped, their seed heads waving. Across the meadow scrubby piñones clothe a rocky hill. The ground underfoot is thick with elk tracks, and you imagine that, were you here in the half hour before dawn, you might glimpse one of the big fellows, nose high, antlers raked back, eyes glaring sidelong at your intrusion, his proud shape melting into the trees.

Yet instantly you appreciate that this place is as sad as it is enchanting. The intermittent stream that once meandered these flats and nourished them with silt now cleaves the meadow in a raw gully twenty-five feet deep. Pines that are decades old grow in it, their tops barely reaching what used to be ground level. You cannot cross the arroyo, not here; you need to search out a better spot, and still you would expect to fill your boots with dirt as you slide down one steep side and scramble up the other, clawing with your hands. Year after year of goats and sheep and milk cows and horses helped to unravel this place, and probably a wagon track once ran down the center of the meadow, preparing a naked strip of earth for storm flows to gnaw away. The final undoing likely came when the all-weather road to the village was built and drainages at the head of the arroyo were rearranged, throwing more runoff into Yerba Anís than it had ever carried before.

There are many things to consider in the meadow. Its open space draws you from the forest and fills you with anticipation. You step past the last trees unthinking. And with those steps you stride through a cluster of five peeled trees that stand almost in a circle, as though they were a committee attesting to the unconsciousness of those who hurry past.

I hurried past those trees for fifteen years never noticing the peels. Each time I passed, I strode into the meadow seeing only the meadow. Usually, after considering the meadow for a moment, I would turn to my left, walk two-dozen paces down-canyon, and take a half-hidden trail climbing the side slope where the canyon narrowed. I cut and cleared that section of trail myself because continued erosion of the arroyo had eaten away the old trail at the edge of the meadow. I cut the trail past two large, orange-barked ponderosas with prominent peels facing each other. I did not notice the peels when I made the trail, but today I cannot walk past them without imagining two Apache women working there, talking, gossiping, passing the time.

The trail I built soon reconnects with the old trail, which then runs along a narrow traverse where the arroyo falls steeply to one side. Thirty paces ahead the canyon widens, its floor flattens, and the going is easy again. This change of habitat is announced by a giant, fat-trunked grandfather ponderosa — the largest tree to be found for a fair distance in any direction. The trail splits at the tree and will take you to either side of it. I like to reach out and pat the scaly bark as I go by. A few score times I expect I have unknowingly patted its peel, which is nearly covered by a regrowth of bark from the edges of the scar. This particular tree began life as a seedling about two hundred years ago and was peeled in 1842. I know this because in 1995 Tom Swetnam and his father, together with the local district ranger and the forest archeologist, paid a visit to my farm and took cores from this and several other trees in the surrounding national forest. A year later, a crew of students from the tree-ring lab took samples from sixteen more trees, together with a dozen trees bearing scars from multiple fires. Another thirty peeled trees were identified but not sampled. All of them stand within a hundred and fifty yards of the main circuit of my walk.

I wish I could say that peeled trees were the only conspicuous things I have lived amid and failed to notice, but alas there is no shortage of objects for my blindness. They exist on multiple levels, in different dimensions. I learn about them too late. My best friend died of an aneurysm in the year before the breakup of my marriage. A blood vessel in his brain burst without warning, and he was felled. I call him my best friend now but would not have called him that then. Not until after he died did I begin to understand how dear his friendship was, how much he meant to me, how much he was in my heart. We got to know each other through work, and as co-workers we saw each other or talked on the phone almost every day for close to six years. He was a remarkable man, invariably thoughtful, constant and unflappable, and by far the funniest human being I have known. I was not so blind as to fail to value his friendship, but the centrality of that relationship in my life, its vital importance, somehow crept up on me without my understanding and acknowledging it — until he died, and grief removed a cataract from my eyes. Then it became easier to see that love can grow like forest trees, slowly but massively, its evidence surrounding you like peeled trees that you fail to see, even though you touch them daily. Sometimes, too, love can die that way, in slow increments, turning into the things that love is not, things that cluster invisibly around you like peeled trees, until finally you see them, and then you see little else.

The earliest peel date that Tom Swetnam and his students recovered from the trees along the walk was 1776, the year of the Declaration of Independence. The ponderosa from which it was taken was already almost two centuries old when Indians — probably Jicarilla Apaches — scraped its bark away. The ring-counters at Swetnam's laboratory determined that it had formed its pith as a seedling within a year or two of 1588, a decade before Juan de Oñate founded the first Spanish colony in New Mexico. Oñate's expedition was a chapter of human experience closer in time and spirit to the late Crusades than to our own. These mountains were then swaddled in myth. History had barely touched them.

But history was hard at work here in 1877, the latest of the peel dates recorded from these woods. Apaches were scarce in the forests by then but not absent. An old-timer from Las Trampas, now long departed, who was born in 1900, said that when he was young, Indians — it wasn't clear if they were Jicarilla Apaches or Pueblos from Picurís, but the two groups had a long, deep association — still came occasionally to trade with villagers along the Río de las Trampas. They were good potters, said Tranquilino Lopez, and they traded the pots they made to village farmers for food. The rules of exchange were elegantly simple. A small, ornamented pot might be traded for the volume of lard it would hold. A large plain olla, by contrast, passed hands for its volume in flour.

The dates for peeling that Tom Swetnam and his students determined from the samples they collected here did not cluster in any particular period between 1776 and 1877. More of them fell late in the period rather than early, but it is easy to ascribe that imbalance to the steady loss of large old trees, whether from logging or other causes. In general, our little study seemed to indicate that far from providing emergency food during periods of famine, the pines of our forest were peeled with regularity over a long span. I like to imagine that a good deal of the tree peeling was carried out by bands who came to trade their pots for lard and flour, as old Tranquilino described. It is easy to imagine them camped in the uneroded meadows of Yerba Anís, secluded along the river trail between the downstream village of Las Trampas and the upstream village of El Valle, where my farm and cabin lie. The meadows would have afforded proximity to water, privacy from the villages, and grazing for horses. But I have found no teepee rings in the meadows themselves, so I regard my hypothesis as flimsy. For all anyone knows, the trees peeled in this forest were peeled not by visiting nomads but by the villagers themselves, who over the span of generations probably included a fair number of Apache slaves and servants, any of whom might have known the practice and passed it on to others. But all of this is speculation. You can spin these and other related facts into any number of patterns that aspire to explain the testimony of the landscape. All of them are plausible; none can yet be proved, nor probably ever will be.

One thing sticks in my mind, though. An archeologist friend calls it the KOA principle: a good place to camp is a good place to camp is a good place to camp. The junction of Arroyo Yerba Anís and the Río de las Trampas is such a place. A few families of Jicarilla might well have used it, and perhaps if they camped close to the river subsequent floods might have rearranged the telltale rings of stones they would have used to keep the bottom edge of their teepees from flapping. In more recent times the site also appealed to a band of latter-day nomads, who fancied living large and wild. These atavists, who called themselves the Banditos, camped for several weeks beside the sandy delta of Yerba Anís during the heady high tide of hippiedom, sometime around 1969 or 1970.

They were not sentimental flower children. They liked guns. Some carried knives and knew how to use them for more than whittling and cooking. A few were running from the law. And they had reason to keep running. They poached big game. They dealt hard drugs. They did not concern themselves with other people's rules. When a few of them had an argument with a friend of mine in Las Trampas, they wrecked his place and cut down his fruit trees, like Carson punishing the Navajo. They were locally famous enough to get written up in a feature story in *Rolling Stone*. The article portrayed them as romantic, modern-day outlaws of the Wild West. The outlaw part was certainly true. One of their more noteworthy exploits occurred high in the heart of the Pecos Wilderness beside a headwater stream of the Río Pecos called Jarosa Creek. Late one morning in midsummer, a wilderness ranger rode by their camp and noticed fresh elk and deer skins. Summer was not a legal hunting season.

A few days later when a game warden and the local district ranger showed up to ask questions, one or two Banditos reached quickly for weapons and got the drop on them. The agency people had the good sense not to try anything heroic, although the game warden was wearing a pistol, and no shots were fired. While the leader of the Banditos, who became known in Forest Service folklore as Two-Braid, trained a cocked rifle on the chest of the warden, the rest of the band hastily packed the best of their gear and hung it on the backs of their horses. In twos and threes they slipped away in multiple directions. When the last of the others were out of sight, Two-Braid mounted a horse and trotted away, turning in the saddle to keep his rifle pointed at the government men until the forest closed around him. A backcountry manhunt ensued, but the only candidate for arrest any of the authorities found was a sweet-faced young woman riding a barefoot mare along a far-off ridge with a colt trailing behind. She said she knew nothing about poached game and less about a showdown on Jarosa Creek. The lawmen did not bother to bring her in. Survivors of the Banditos still live in the area. Of the several who did not survive the ensuing years, I know of only one who died of natural causes. The bones, or rather the ashes, of one of them are still in the mountains.

When the Banditos camped at the mouth of Yerba Anís and a few years later when I first saw the place, it was an open, scoured expanse of sand, gravel, and cobble lightly clothed in grasses and a few shrubs. Today, after a long reprieve from livestock, it has become a jungle of willows, alders, and young cottonwoods. I go there on my walks and struggle to visualize how it used to look. It is like trying to remember what I was like back then. I sort through memories that are fragmentary and as often revisionist and self-protective as they are honest and true. Much of the truth of those days is like the truth of the origin of the peeled trees, lost down a river of time. I can say that I wish I had taken more pictures or that I wish I had taken more notes, but I am not sure I really do. Having practiced the historian's trade, I sometimes feel overwhelmed by the prolixity of the archives of the world, and I can say with certainty that neither the world nor I needs archives of me. Sometimes the best thing to do with the past is to let it go. At least, that is what the river seems to say.

The river is beside me now. At the junction of the river and the arroyo, near the old Bandito campsite, I turn upstream along the main canyon trail. The wind-whispering silence of the forest and of Arroyo Yerba Anís dissolves before the incessant growl of the Río de las Trampas, the River of Traps.

I feel the water drumming at my mind even before I see it. *Síste víator!* I stop and listen.

River speech is a concatenation of murmurs and burbles, hisses and humming, snarls, chokes, whispered asides, and violent coughs. The voice of mountain water is always many voices, blended like the roar of a crowd, and although even before you think about it you know that you can never tease those myriad elements apart, you keen your ears, leaning forward, wondering, Which of all those voices speaks to me?

The Río de las Trampas is my river, my enigma, my puzzle, my koan. Its waters have nourished me, bathed me, washed my children, and irrigated my fields. I have fought its floods and grieved through its droughts. I have studied it, stared at it, stepped in it, written about it, slipped in it, sat in it, splashed and been splashed by it, slept by it, strolled and stalked by it, stormed across it and sidled back. It has been in my dreams and in my waking thoughts more than any other inanimate thing I have known, and the better I know it, the less I am convinced it is inanimate. When I am alone I talk to it, and sometimes it seems to talk back. I have a rule that every time I come to the farm, even if for only a few minutes to pick something up or drop something off, I must take time to walk down to the river, say hello, and pay my respects. In twenty-seven years, or however long it has been, I have broken that rule a few times, and I am certain that on each occasion I have been punished for the breach.

Trampas means traps, and a lot of people understandably think that the traps in question were beaver traps. These mountains once abounded in the big rodents, and they were the first range in the Southwest to be ransacked by the so-called Mountain Men of the Rocky Mountain fur trade. But the village of Las Trampas and the creek running through it acquired their names several generations before gringos began hauling beaver pelts back to Saint Louis, and until then there had been no appreciable trade in fine furs in the warm-weather Spanish province of New Mexico. In my first years here I asked every old-timer who would talk to me what the namesake traps of the area might have snared. Nobody knew. "They just always call it that" was the usual answer, although one grinning lecher answered my question about what was trapped with a hopeful query of his own: "Maybe women?"

I have wondered if the box canyon through which the river runs between Las Trampas and El Valle might have served as a kind of trap for game drives, but I suspect that while such an explanation serves logic, it fails entirely to honor the qualities of accident and serendipity that lie behind the naming of most places. The name *Las Trampas* might just as easily have come about because some early traveler noticed a couple of rabbit snares, or something that looked like rabbit snares, when he paused at the river to get a drink of water. No matter what was trapped in the past, the river is still a place of traps. It has sure enough caught me. I have at times lived far from its banks since I first met it, but I have not lived happily in those places. I am stuck. I have to be here. Not all the time, but frequently. Otherwise I am like Ishmael when he's been too long away from the sea. I grow gloomy, and before long the gloominess grows surly. I come to the banks of the Trampas to set myself right. That's the way it is.

Sometimes it helps to go to the edge of the river and squat down and watch how the clear water curls and gurgles over a rounded boulder in an open stretch of stream. Looking closely, you see striations in the current as it swells over the rock. They gleam like fine hair. If you tried to paint them, you would have to use the most delicate and transparent colors and a gossamer brush. The boulder is rounded smooth but not by water. More likely, its fine polish is the work of one of the pocket glaciers that sat at the headwaters of this stream throughout most of the Pleistocene. The cirque that successive glaciers carved is fourteen miles upstream. The boulder has come that far in thirteen thousand or maybe thirty thousand years. It is still traveling.

I have stood beside the flooding river when boulders like that have been on the move. I have heard them clack ominously as they collide unseen beneath the dark roiling water. Once, in flood-related emergency, I had to wade into the river amid the clacking boulders. A rope around my waist and tied to a post kept me from being swept away, but the boulders made me worry for my feet and legs. That night, an army of boulders clacked in my dreams, and water rushed darkly around me. I imagine that if water could dream, it would dream of the ocean, where it is always trying to go. I imagine too that if boulders could dream, they would dream no less for the ocean, but they would dream incomprehensibly slowly, and they would dream of themselves as sand.

In the last weeks the weather has warmed and the river has swollen with snowmelt, enough so that water now streams over the top of the boulder I am looking at, and a tiny recirculating wave keeps forming in the mini-rapid of its lee. But the wave cannot hold. It quivers an inch upstream, then quivers an inch down. It shudders and vanishes, then reappears and quivers some more. It is the apotheosis of instability, trembling with constant change. This tiny drama, repeated at every boulder, stone, and log in the river, becomes in the aggregate a river-long throbbing that is infinite in the variety of its expression and the continuity of its permanence. Or maybe I should not call it a throbbing but a vibration, or not a vibration but a grumbling, because it is audible. Or not a grumbling but a kind of deep-throated laughter. The marvel is that this sound, whether whispered or shouted, has voiced itself continuously in this canyon for tens of thousands of years, maybe hundreds of thousands. The river has never ceased to speak.

I leave the boulder and continue upstream along the walk. River sound fills my ears. I climb the natural stair steps of an outcrop of granite that juts to the edge of the stream. The outcrop is what remains of a stone ledge that once spanned the river and probably made a waterfall. The river long ago breached this barrier and washed it away, but a remnant bed of granite still retards the river's flow and makes it form a pool. Waist-deep and two or three body lengths across, it is the largest pool in this reach of the river. We call it the Swimming Hole.

Many a summer day I have played here with my children and with the children of neighbors and friends. They wade and splash in the cold mountain water, they float sticks in the current to worry the dogs and dabble their toes from the water-smooth rocks where the current rushes in. They bring rocks to build a low porous dam that raises the level of the pool. The name we have given the place is of course an exaggeration — it is much too small for swimming — and in my experience the water is warm enough to invite full immersion only for a handful of days in late July and August. Nevertheless, it is the wettest, coolest, and most welcoming summer oasis we have.

But it is not welcoming the rest of the year, least of all now as the river swells with snowmelt. Viewed from the granite shelf above the pool, it is dark with depth, cold and menacing. Runoff from the mountain snowpack has made it broader and brawnier than it has been for years, and it has swept away last summer's dam of rocks. The dabbling rocks where bathers bask are drowned in cold swirling water. The river is turbulent and frothy; its currents churn with waves that slap the rocks, collide with other waves, splash up, fall back, and form again out of a black swirl. Two major currents flow here. The water coursing nearest me pours into the pool, shoots down a line of white-capped standing waves, and surges out the breach where the dam has given way.

The other current does not escape the pool. The farther half of the onrushing stream pours crashing in, but the standing waves shoulder it aside. It veers and turns on itself. It gyres into a deep, froth-topped eddy, dark and cold, that cycles and circles, round and round, corkscrewing inexorably to the black, down-sucking center. I stare into it, transfixed. The eddy spirals and spins. If I look away, the stationary land seems to be in motion, unwinding the coil of the eddy. I look back at the dervishing pool. I see in the eddy the embodiment of irresolution — everything pulled round in a cold circle, nothing escaping. It is like a mind, trapped in its thoughts, unable to let go of what troubles it. It is like the 3 A.M. mind of an insomniac, churning while the body tosses, conjugating regrets and errors, mourning the massed deaths of possibility. It is like my mind, most nights since early winter, now that my marriage has come apart.

The eddy can also stand for a certain kind of relationship with which I am familiar, a relationship without outlet or progress, a relationship in which old patterns cycle without change or growth, in which movement shrinks inward to the tightest part of the spiral, reduced finally to spinning in place.

The high-water eddy of the Swimming Hole may be the truest namesake of the River of Traps. Anything caught in it could be caught a very long time, drowning in repetition, circling round and round, observed only by the lidless eyes of a hungry trout, which finally with a swirl of fins and a lightning bite gives the eddying morsel its deliverance. A 3 A.M. mind prays for deliverance of any kind. It whips back and forth between the bleak desire for destructive surcease and the frail hope that somehow, kicking and flailing, it might pierce the border of the eddy and shoot free into the violent, ocean-bound flow that roars through the pool and crashes downstream toward a future. Even that, however, is an imperfect balm for a mind inclined toward melancholy. Pursuing a future means releasing the past, which then becomes final and irrevocable, its regrets beyond repair.

The eddy swirls hypnotically. The grumbling low boom of wave thunder feels lulling, sedative. On this day a chill breeze chases the snowmelt waters down the canyon, and the Swimming Hole offers not enchantment but a meaner kind of seduction. It leads toward heaviness and anesthesia, toward paralysis of heart and mind. This must be what the ancients felt when they conjured the waters of Lethe. It takes all my strength and concentration to muster the will to stand and face into the wind and take the trail once more, which I do with leaden heart, and continue upstream toward the mill.

The ruins are plain. Even an eye that fails to notice peeled trees cannot ignore the odd arrangement of low posts and rotted palings that lie beside the canyon trail. The purpose that the ruins served, however, remained for me a mystery until a neighbor told their story. Jacobo Romero lived at the next farm up the valley and was a mentor, teacher, and friend for a decade. When he died in 1986, he was a little older than the century. He'd grown up in a world in which only Spanish was spoken, and it was rarely written down. In the world of Jacobo's childhood, knowledge passed from generation to generation not so much through books as through stories told person to person, face to face, voice to ear. Schooled in what ethnologists call the oral tradition, Jacobo became a master storyteller himself, and he loved to recall the evenings of his youth, sitting near corner fireplaces in homes of spartan simplicity, when he listened to the *ancianos* — the old ones — weave their stories of the past.

More than once he heard the story of the settling of El Valle, and more than once he passed the story on. He said that settlers from Las Trampas cultivated grain in the valley long before they built shelters here and still longer before they came to live permanently. They began by digging the first of the valley's three main irrigation ditches. This was the *acequia abajo*, the lower ditch, which waters a few hundred acres in the downstream half of the valley, including my land. Jacobo said he'd heard that my fields were meadows when the settlers came to them. The rest of the arable land was clothed in forest and had to be cleared. The Trampeseños planted the lands served by the acequia abajo in oats, barley, and wheat. They harvested the grain with sickles and hauled it back to Las Trampas on the backs of burros.

In time, they built a mill rather than haul so much bulk through the canyon. When Jacobo told me of the mill, he was nearly eighty years old. He still worked in his fields every day, but arthritis in his knees kept him from walking long distances. He said, "If you want to see it, it's just there in the cañoncito between the river and the trail, not very far from your gate."

That was more than twenty years ago. Today the ruins are markedly more disintegrated than when I first saw them, especially the remains of a hollowed log that may have served as a flume. Now it is hard to tell that the few slabs of rotting wood were ever much of a log at all. But the rest of the mill — three of the four cedar corner posts and the remnants of a dozen poles that were part of a low barrier of palings facing the river — are more or less as they were in the 1970s. The contour of the ground tells more of the story. The mill is centered in a little swale, which its builders probably dug. Immediately upstream is a low mound — the earth they excavated from the swale. The remains of the putative flume lie along the slope of the mound. A ditch would have brought water to the mouth of the flume, and the water would have shot down the flume at a strong angle and hit the mill's waterwheel with heavy force.

The mill itself would have been a log shack built on a platform atop the corner posts. No sign of such logs remains there today; probably they were carried off by floodwaters or put to new uses when the mill was abandoned. The waterwheel lay underneath the platform in the space created by the swale. Hung horizontally, it would have turned a simple vertical axle that ran up through the platform, then through the center of a stationary millstone to which it was not attached and which it did not turn, and then to a second millstone with a squared center hole, which the shaft of the axle fit exactly. The water turned the upper millstone, which rotated atop the stationary one. Grain was fed between them, and a mixture of flour and bran, soon to be separated by sifting, was the result.

Years ago when Tom Swetnam came to El Valle and took the first samples from peeled trees along the walk, he also sampled timbers from the ruins of the mill. Only two of the samples yielded a date, which was probably reliable but not scientifically certain: 1816, a year that fits what little is known of the valley's distant past. Las Trampas was officially founded in 1751, when the governor of the province of Nuevo Mexico awarded the Trampas Land Grant to twelve heads of families from the poorest barrio in Santa Fe. Their chief was a man already advanced in years, Juan de Arguello, who led his fellow settlers to their new, wild mountain home, where they dug acequias, laid out fields, and soon began building their houses, connecting them wall-to-wall in the form of a fortified plaza, together with a massive adobe church, anchoring one side of the plaza, which stands today.

The settlers' church, the mission of Santo Tomás Apostól de las Trampas, is a glorious thing. No finer example of Spanish colonial mission architecture exists in all of New Mexico. But it appears that Las Trampas got its start even before the governor issued the 1751 grant. Still more research by Swetnam's lab tells us that the Trampeseños incorporated timbers in the construction of the church that had been cut ten or fifteen years earlier. It makes sense that Juan de Arguello, his sons, and compatriots might have built a stockade or at least a stout cabin in the years before legal settlement. In such a place they might have laid plans for their village beside the river and the farms they would carve from the woods and meadows. If so, it was a place of hard-tempered dreams, of a kind of iron-willed hope taking root in defiance of steep and dangerous odds.

The Trampas valley in those days was a bloody ground. Comanches from the plains frequently crossed the mountains to prey upon Pueblo and Spanish settlements along the Río Grande and its tributaries, especially the Río Santa Cruz. French traders from Louisiana provided them with more and better guns than the Spanish had, and thus armed, the Comanche supplemented their bison-based economy with horses, sheep, and cattle stolen from New Mexico. They also plied a vigorous trade in captive women and children. In the middle decades of the eighteenth century the colony of New Mexico was like a farm from which they harvested crops of animals and human beings virtually at will. From the colony's point of view, the Comanches were devils, and the hold they maintained on New Mexico was like the grip of a python. They squeezed the colony so tightly that it could not expand; it could scarcely breathe.

Settlements like Las Trampas were intended to remedy the

situation. They drained population from Santa Fe, which was hard-pressed to feed its people, and they presented an additional, if tenuous, barrier to Comanches ranging along their favorite routes of ingress to the colony. It was a harsh, tough bargain for the Trampeseños, which the settlers accepted without illusion. In exchange for land, they fought for their lives. They were pawns in the great struggle of their day and region, not cannon fodder exactly but something akin to musket or arrow fodder. They bled, but they hung on. Virtually nothing is known of what the Trampeseños experienced in the early decades of their village—the skirmishes they fought, the casualties they suffered, the rapes and abductions, the hunger when crops failed or stock was driven off, the acts of vengeance. Records do not exist. History must judge, however, that they gave as good as they got. Their community survived. They clung to the rocks and tree roots of their cold, rugged valley, and they did not give up.

Nor did they venture far afield—for a while. The Comanche grip on New Mexico remained too strong, at least until 1779 when one of the Southwest's most remarkable men changed the fortunes of the colony and of Las Trampas. Don Juan Bautista de Anza lived his life in the saddle. By one estimate he rode forty thousand miles in his short life of forty-five years. In 1776 he led an expedition of Sonoran colonists across the continent's most forbidding deserts to found a new settlement on San Francisco Bay. It was his second trip; he'd pioneered the route a year earlier. Soon thereafter he came to New Mexico, ostensibly as governor of the colony but effectively as its general. He came to kill the Comanche python.

Several sons of Las Trampas may have been among the Pueblo and Hispanic militia that augmented his small command of professional soldiers. Where the plains of southeastern Colorado meet the foothills of the Rockies, his forces collided with the greater part of the Comanche nation, led by a chief who wore on his head a single bison horn painted green. This was Cuerno Verde, Green Horn, and the mountain that looms above the site of the battle is today known as Greenhorn Peak.

Anza did not rush to battle. He feinted, tempted, and drew in the Comanche force. Then he crushed it. When the din of battle ceased, Cuerno Verde's body was among those that littered the field. It would be wrong to call the years that followed a period of peace for New Mexico—the Comanches by no means disappeared, and the Navajos, Utes, and various bands of Apaches made their presence felt—but it was something closer to peace than anything the colony had previously experienced. Villages like Las Trampas began to stretch their limbs without fear of amputation. The settlers made increasing use of neighboring valleys: Ojo Sarco, Vallecitos, Chamisal, El Valle. And in time the men and women who farmed El Valle built a mill.

Building that mill was as much an act of hope as Anza's expedition to San Francisco or Arguello's to Las Trampas. The great Czech leader and playwright, Václav Havel, has written,

"Hope is not a feeling. It is not the belief that things will turn out well, but the conviction that what we are doing makes sense, no matter how things turn out." Havel should know. He battled the Soviets for many years and against great odds. When the Soviet empire finally crumbled, he battled anew through the birth throes and bickering of the new Czech nation, which he served as president. He did not give up that struggle either, though he could have done so with honor and though it cost him his health. Through years of peril and labor, he clung to a species of hope that was based not on an expectation of outcome — of achieving instrumental good, for in fact, the odds, coldly calculated, favored defeat — but on a visceral faith that good inhered in what he was doing, that it was intrinsic, and that because of it, what he was doing was right and necessary whether it succeeded or not.

People whose character and community formed under the shadow of Comanche depredation would not have sat before their fireplaces arguing the merits of instrumental versus intrinsic good as Aquinas, Augustine, or Havel might have done, but they would have felt the difference in their hearts. They were more familiar with failure than success. They eked out a spare existence from stingy fields and a harsh, capricious climate. They had almost no metal. A knife or a nail was a precious thing. They fashioned their plows from burls of fire-hardened oak to furrow the rocky soil. Books and literacy were dreams; wax for candles a luxury. They worked and feuded, wooed, loved and grieved, sinned and suffered each other's sinning, ached, prayed, and exulted all within the narrow compass of the Río de las Trampas and its enfolding ridges. They were manifestly imperfect people, like the rest of us, but on a day in 1816, having mustered a collection of crude, dull, and inefficient tools, some of them gathered in the river canyon at an advantageous site beside a trail that was already ancient and began to build a mill.

It is a sure bet that they chose their site wisely. In almost thirty years of irrigation, I have spent enough time with a shovel in my hands to have a pretty good idea of what it is to eye a project and calculate the simplest and easiest way to carry it off. People who dig a lot learn how to dig less. They gauge the roll and slope of the land so that they win their goal with the least amount of excavation. I say this as a beneficiary of tempered steel. Imagine the devotion to saved effort of a people for whom low-grade iron was scarce and the wood of scrub oaks the hardest other tool-making thing they had.

But if all this is true — and it cannot reasonably be otherwise — we have a mystery to solve. The ruins may once have been in a good site for a mill, but they are no longer so. I calculate that in order to deliver a head of flowing water to the mill, the bed of the river in the time of the mill builders would have had to be eight to ten feet higher than it is today. Unless the riverbed were higher, the ditch that served as the millrace would have had to wrap around the waist of a granite abutment of the canyon, much like the abutment that helps to form the Swimming Hole, and then extend more than a hundred and fifty yards upstream. Such a ditch would have required a great deal of digging, and the passage around the abutment would have required construction of an aqueduct. It is undiggable; there is no soil, no sand, gravel, or even cobble to remove, only monolithic granite. In terms of the present bed of the river and contours of the canyon, one could hardly pick a worse site for a mill than the location of the ruins.

Something catastrophic and transformative must have occurred, but I don't know what it was. All I have is conjecture: that the granite abutment that would defeat the excavation of a millrace formerly extended its foot across the path of the river and formed a ledge; that this ledge was the feature that attracted the mill builders to the site because it created the drop, the hydraulic head, they needed; that the original millrace started at the ledge and led no more than two dozen yards to the mill; that a flood of stunning proportions long ago tore out the ledge and rendered the mill useless; that the reach of river through the lower valley, including my land, is still lowering its bed in slow adjustment to the impact of that distant flood.

Fast change and slow change, violent flood and the subsequent quiet resorting and shifting of materials, are like two brothers. One gestures boldly, throws wild parties, and leaves a mess; he also draws the world's attention. The other stays home, reads a lot, cleans up after his more dramatic sib, and continually putters around the house. No one notices how the house is slowly transformed. More and more I find myself fascinated by the quiet one, and by the idea that this pair of brothers inhabits more than just rivers. Everything about rivers has some kind of parallel in human life. They are the richest source of metaphor in all of nature, and for obvious reasons. They brim with life, as we do; they are as vocal as we are; their moods are endlessly variable, as ours are; and their ceaseless flow duplicates our sense of time. Nothing we can observe in landscape is more riveting than a river in full flood, rampaging and muscular, sweeping all before it. Yet a flood is episodic, and slow change is working all the time.

I've seen the Río de las Trampas flood twice in my time here. I don't mean days of high runoff when the stream leaks outside its usual channel and roars so loud you hear it at night inside the house. That kind of water, while not usual, is not rare; in semi-arid country like this, one learns to welcome it as a harbinger of plenty. A real flood tears apart the riverbanks, reshapes the channel, and sets the boulders clacking. A real flood roars so loud you hear it in your dreams. The first one I saw came in May 1979 and lasted a week. All that week and the week before, sustained, heavy rain fell on a deep, warming snowpack. Rain and snowmelt joined in a volume the river had not carried in a generation or more. The river tore at its banks, ripped out the bridge of the county road midway up the valley, and swept away every fence, log, and footbridge that crossed it. The gashed, eroded meadows it left behind, ending in torn banks of dripping, raw earth and exposed tree roots, presented one of the sorriest sights I have seen. It seemed the land was ruined, fatally scarred, that it would never recover its beauty. But in time it did.

The second flood slashed down the valley during a downpour in July 1998. It was not as powerful or as long-lasting as the 1979 event, but the torrent still ripped the grassy skin from the banks and carried off god knows how many hundreds of tons of good dark mountain soil. It also swept away the footbridge I had built, which stood three and a half feet above the normal surface of the water. This time I was prepared, however. I had tethered the bridge to a burly cottonwood with a stout chain. When the flood ebbed, the bridge lay on a sandbar still intact with the chain stretched taut. It took three days to set a new pier of juniper posts where the bank had eroded and, with the help of a friend, to winch the bridge back in place. Each of these floods seemed to set new dynamics of slow change in motion. I've watched patches of river bottom change from cobbles to gravel to sand and back to cobbles again. I've watched plugs — aggregations of gravel and small cobbles — migrate slowly downriver. I have watched the bed of the river gradually incise into its substrate so that today its absolute elevation through my land is at least a foot lower than when I started taking the walk.

Or rather, I *think* I have seen these things. I cannot be sure. The changes are slow and incremental, and I have never troubled to install the kinds of transects that would allow me to measure the dynamics of the stream channel with precision. Maybe I should do that now, or soon. Slow change eludes measurement. Fast change loudly declares itself at every turn, but slow change scarcely speaks. It is the brother who reads and naps by day and tinkers with the house while others sleep. Unless I ask exactly the right question, he will not tell me what he does, let alone what he thinks. And he fiddles with so many things, the river being only one of them. I think about the fast change of my friend's sudden death. It was no less catastrophic than the sweeping away of a river ledge. And then I think about the slow change it set in motion, the sorting and rechanneling of the lives he touched, mine included. My friend was as devoted a family man as ever lived, and he would be appalled to know that as a consequence of the emptiness he left behind, another kind of emptiness became still more apparent to me, but there it is: slow change worked its way, and gradually the fabric of my marriage unraveled.

There is another element to add to the story of the mill and its mysterious, impossible location. We think the mill was built about 1816. In 1821 Mexico declared its independence from Spain and opened its borders. That year, William Becknell led the first trade caravan from Missouri to Santa Fe, and the commerce of the Santa Fe Trail soon flourished. The muleskinners who tended Becknell's caravan carried beaver traps in their kits. When Becknell returned eastward across the plains with bags of rawhide shrunk around silver pesos, most of his men stayed behind, and they soon spread into the mountains nearest to Santa Fe and Taos, stripping the beaver from the streams as other trappers had been doing in the northern Rockies for more than a decade.

Although few, if any, beavers inhabit the Río de las Trampas today, it is likely that two hundred years ago a fair number—and perhaps many—of the soggy, industrious rodents maintained dams and lodges in the valley. The villagers probably killed them on sight—no one wanted them clotting up headgates and irrigation ditches with their sticks, let alone flooding riverside pastures and grain fields—but in the higher, wilder reaches of the river, the creatures probably lived unmolested. If so, they would have strongly influenced the hydrology of the river, moderating its flows with their chains of ponds, spreading floodwaters over broad areas, and arresting any tendency of the stream to incise its channel.

If the beaver were present, and then suddenly they were not—because Anglo trappers, the so-called Mountain Men, rapidly and efficiently captured lodge after lodge—what would have been the effect on the river? Without living beavers to maintain and replace them, the dams would decay and eventually break; the ponds would drain; the moderating influence of the miles-long chain of beaver works would slowly wane. With the amplitude of floods having been so long suppressed, would the system's vulnerability to ordinary events now greatly increase? Would extreme events now produce catastrophe? It is tempting to speculate that as a consequence of the independence of Mexico from Spain, the ledge that served the first gristmill in El Valle washed away. The links between that cause and its distant environmental effect in a remote valley are tenuous and particular, yet history and our lives are shaped by many chains of cause and effect that are no less tenuous and particular, no less mysterious and obscure. Václav Havel understood this and knew that because of it, the hopes that guide us, if they are to be durable, must be intrinsic and not instrumental; they must be robust enough to withstand the vagaries of chance setbacks and reversals, sudden floods and unpredicted sorrows. The hopes of the farmers of El Valle were robust in this way. When changes in the river destroyed the usefulness of their mill, they hopefully built another, at a better site farther upstream.

At last, I have reached the canyon mouth. Here is the fence, the gate, the meadow canopied by graceful, arching cotton-woods. Home. I leave behind the ruins of the mill, the pink granite abutment of the canyon side, the territory of Carson National Forest. I step through the gate into land I am said to own, though I feel more owned than owning. It seems a funny thing to claim ownership of something that will outlive me and is essentially immortal, but I will put that thought aside. Here I am at the fence that crosses the river at the canyon mouth, which every flood and a few high-water snowmelts have car-ried away and which I have rebuilt at least four times, but I lose count. Here I am beside a ponderosa pine growing from the riverbank, which the flood of 1979 so undercut that the pine tipped riverward like the mast of a heeling ship. I was sure the tree was doomed and waited for it to topple or die. It did neither, and still grows.

I should take the tree for an example, I tell myself. Persevere. Stand as fast as I am able. My mind is still beset with the turmoil of the Swimming Hole: the dark, relentless swirl of the eddy, the violent rupture of the straight-through current. Hopefulness is the antidote, but not every variety of hope will confer it. The civilization-building hope shared by Václav Havel and the builders of the mill seems an abstract and distant thing. The kind of hope I need is humbler and more personal.

I remember another day when I stood in this spot. It was winter. Two inches of snow had fallen, snow that was unimaginably cold and light. I took the walk at dawn. The white forest was immaculate and still. Where Arroyo Yerba Anís joins the river canyon, where the coldest air had settled, I crossed the track of an ermine. The faint footprints, in sets of three, described a weaselly lope, the fourth foot landing on the track of the second. A little farther along, I turned upstream along the ice-hung river and soon rounded a bend to face the rising sun head-on.

The low wild light came bowling down the canyon, forcing its brilliance through the shadowed limbs of the riverside trees. The sky was already as blue as a robin's egg, and the merest breath of air brushed snow from the high branches of the trees. Flake by flake, the snow wafted down, sparkling like motes of cold fire. I passed the Swimming Hole, where the river gurgled under a sheet of ice. I passed the ruins of the mill, the air still drizzling with snow gems. I came through the gate to my pasture, and the widening spaces of the river meadow presented a scene of even greater enchantment. Snow flocked the up-reaching branches of the cottonwoods, and the pale gray trunks were almost as white. They stretched skyward, gently leaning toward each other in an architecture that seemed musical, as through they were the notes of a sweet, harmonic chord. The snow-blanketed ground was a kind of bass tone, steady and untracked, not a tuft of grass poking through. The crystalline air magnified the sunrise into a glory that chimed inside the mind like a bell. *Siste viator.* I stopped at the edge of the meadow.

The shortest way back to the cabin lay straight ahead, through the cottonwoods and then up through the hayfield gate. But I could not go forward. The scene was too exqui-site, too fragile to enter. I briefly debated running the long way around the fields to fetch a camera and hurrying back, but the beauty of the moment would not last the time the errand would take, and I did not want to lose the mood of stillness and revelation that had captured me. The sun was rising. The angle of its light and the temperature of the air were creeping upward by increments that would soon trans-form the snowflakes and airborne crystals of what seemed pure light. The scene would last in this purity only minutes more. I watched a while, then turned away, not waiting to see it fade.

A species of hope resides in such moments. What gives hope is not so much the outward perfection of beauty as the fact that we can perceive it, and if we behold beauty today, might tomorrow not give us something as rare and pure? This is real inspiration—it blows spirit into us—and to feel the spirit enter is to know the hopeful possibility that it may reenter many times more. But no matter how great a blessing such hope may be, it is a fragile thing, for it depends on something outside of us: the thing perceived, the moment of perfection. This is not a small point. There is a difference between receiving the gift of inspiration from an external source and somehow generating it from within. When one seeks a durable hope, only the latter will do.

Many of the hopes we carry within us, from the quotidian to the extraordinary, depend on outcomes we do not control. We say to ourselves, I hope I get the job, the raise, the promotion. I hope she likes me, loves me, forgives me. I hope for the happiness of my family, my friends, my community. The larger the circle of outcomes grows, the less of it we control: we hope our nation will live the truth of its ideals. That is a call to a lifetime of work, and it begins with the hope that individually we might do the same. Even when we are the principal actor, we know we must live with uncertainty. Exigencies and emergencies will converge. Contingencies will assert their influence. We say, I hope I can recover my health, my peace of mind, my faith. Reaching still higher, we may hope to approach the mystery, to feel the beauty passing through, to glimpse the who and why of what we are amid the enormity of all that we are not. Such aspiration can lift us high, but only when our weight is light.

The trouble, at least for me, is that when I most need hope, I am as heavy as stones.

In the darkest times we search for what is durable, for a hope that does not melt like snowflakes and that does not depend on external energies or even on our own good behavior. One day, on the walk, I thought I touched such a hope.

My horse had died. It was the same spring when I stared into the dark eddy of the Swimming Hole and saw how the straight-through current had torn apart the children's dam. It was the spring following the winter when my family came apart. And then came the death of my horse.

He was a ranch-raised gelding from south-central New Mexico near Cuchillo, in the dry, rocky country that drains from the Black Range to the Río Grande. I had bought him a couple of years earlier from a cowboy and horse trainer I trusted, after a long search. A good horse is as hard to find as a friend. There has to be a fit. Horses have as many habits, good and bad, as people do. Some have a work ethic; some don't. Some have a sense of humor; some don't. It takes more than one ride to find out about a horse. Sometimes it takes years.

Smokey came by his name honestly. He was a grulla, which along with buckskin and dun is called a native color. A herd of mustangs, left alone, will breed toward native colors over time. Grulla is a dark purple, the color of smoke with a tinge of red. Smokey's coat graded to black at the stockings. His mane and tail were black, and he had a black stripe down his lower spine, which recalled the pelage of the last wild horses of Asia and

Eastern Europe. He was medium height, thick-boned and muscular; he had the right body for mountain work. His hooves were hard and black, and when he walked, his feet moved straight in line with no looping out or in. Loose rock or slick river bottoms did not trouble him. He took good care of his feet and remained calm in conditions that would start many another horse to lunge or buck. He was as gentle as a dog and liked the company of humans, though he was hell on other horses and always fought to be king of the corral. There was nothing fancy about him. He did not have the fast walk or silky trot that made the miles drop effortlessly away, and he was not as exciting a ride as some of the fierier horses I have had, but he was a mount that would keep the two of us out of trouble on long solitary rides in rough country, and he was a friend.

From winter through the first half of the summer of 2002, a drought gripped New Mexico. It was so harsh that the grass did not green in El Valle. My closest neighbor, Jacobo's son Lalo, with whom I shared use of the river pasture, was then dying of lung cancer. He had put a pair of horses in the pasture, and without irrigation the field could not support two horses for long, and certainly not a third. And irrigation soon proved out of the question. I have rights to irrigate that field only when the principal ditches of El Valle and Las Trampas have all the water they need, and that year they did not. Lalo was an old dear friend, and he and I had more important things to talk about than who was going to use what grass. Instead of bringing Smokey home from the ranch where he'd wintered, I trailered him to a ranch for which I was responsible on Rowe Mesa, south of Pecos. I turned Smokey over to Tim Stasel, the solitary cowboy who managed the place, and Tim put Smokey to work as part of his string. We operate that ranch as a grass bank—tending cattle there that normally graze in other places so that those other places can be rested and rehabilitated. All through that summer and into the fall, Smokey worked cattle two or three times a week. I saw him and sometimes rode him when I went up on the mesa to meet with Tim or give him a hand. When winter came, I left him there—because of the drought, I'd grown no hay in El Valle, and I had nothing to feed him. He could stay on the mesa with Tim and get fed in return for the work he'd done.

The spring of 2003 had promise, at least in terms of growing grass. It looked as though the river pasture would green up enough to support Smokey by late April, and I looked forward to bringing him back to the farm and settling into a routine, at least on my days off from regular work, of writing in the morning and riding in the afternoon. I figured those were the best things I could do to keep my balance through a difficult time.

But then Tim called early on the morning of April 7. "I've got to ask you for permission to put Smokey down," he said. It was a clear, dry day. I was just pulling in to the driveway of the house where I had lived with my wife and children, where my office still was. "Yesterday he got quicksanded in the stock tank by headquarters," Tim said. "He bogged real bad in all the silt that's washed in. I don't know how long he was there. Probably no more'n a few hours. But it looked like he'd thrashed around a good deal. Took me a couple more hours to pull him out. I could only pull him by the head, and that's not good. Then he took a wrong step and got stuck again. I had to pull him some more. By the time I got him on hard ground it was already sundown and he was in pretty rough shape."

Somehow Tim managed to put him in a sheltered pen and settle him for the night. He thought maybe Smokey would pull through. But shock and exhaustion can work hard on a horse, and on top of that the pulling and straining must have hurt him. Maybe, too, he had kinked a bowel with his thrashing and brought on a colic, a painful condition for a horse. In the morning Tim went out to find that Smokey had beaten himself senseless against the steel pipe rails of the pen. He was blind for sure and breathing in a shallow, labored rale. That's when Tim telephoned me. I told him, "Do what you have to do."

I went to the farm as soon as I could get away, but the farm seemed a different place. Animation had drained from the landscape. I took the walk, of course. I went up by the Barn Arroyo and over the barren saddle, down through the pines to Arroyo Yerba Anís and the river, then up the river past the Swimming Hole and the ruins of the mill, and home through the gate of the river pasture. By then it was an hour or two past dawn. I had not slept. My mind was in the eddy. The cottonwoods arching over the river were not yet in leaf. In May they would burst with vibrant, bird-filled canopies, but trapped in April they were bare gray poles against the sky. Although the grasses showed a little color, they'd failed to grow much leaf, and the texture of the ground looked worn. Except for the growl of the river, the land was silent. If a jay or a woodpecker called, I did not hear it. The horseless meadow seemed dead.

I walked past the spot, under the cottonwoods, where Anne and I had thrown a party for the whole village when we married, twenty-six years before, and where we'd also picnicked countless times when our children were small. I turned up the path toward the hayfield. Closing the wire gate between the hayfield and the river pasture, I struggled a bit to get the hoop of wire over the gate stay. "I should fix this gate," I thought, and reminded myself, "I am always saying I should fix this gate."

I was facing downhill, looking toward the bend of the river where horses and cattle like to cross. I was in the posture of a moment I had repeated hundreds of times. It is the moment that follows a ride, when I take the horse — any of a dozen horses over all those years — down to the gate of the river pasture, slip off the halter, and let the animal go. Then I close the gate and wait, just to watch. In my mind's eye I see Smokey there, as I put him in the pasture a year and a half earlier, the last time we rode the trails of the walk.

He trots a dozen yards and arches his long neck to look back at me closing the gate. He sees that the human is on the other side of the fence. Nothing more to concern him there. He cranes down to taste the grass before him. He huffs at the ground, paws it a stroke or two, and snuffles the exhalation of the soil: this place smells all right. Smokey gingerly bends to his foreknees, then lets his haunches drop. He lies down on his side, rolls, and becomes an awkward thing, a creature of flight now upended, fleetness forgotten, feet in the air, scratching his back. He pauses, as though to reconsider his abandonment of dignity. Then rolls again. And again. He stands and shivers off the clinging grass and leaves. He looks left, looks right, cocks his ears forward, and cocks them back. His eyes are bright. His equine mind is visibly at work. Done with that, he thinks. Feeling all right now. Feeling fine. He farts loudly and trots down to the creek and then into it, sparks of water flashing. He lunges up the far bank, shod hooves clacking on cobbles. He pauses. Again, he scents the air, nostrils wide. Listens, ears stiff in attention. All clear. Well, then: *yes!* He snorts, tosses his head, and sprints into the open meadow, neck bowed, tail high, mane blown back. He runs, flat-out. He reaches for the horizon with every stride. The field, irrigated in those days, is soft, compliant. His hooves and legs feel good. His muscles stretch and exult. He bucks, kicking high and on the run, hind legs striking at nothing. Or rather, striking at any contradiction of his present independence. He can run, free and fast. He can *be* speed. He can *be* all horse.

I watch as Smokey flattens, going faster, sod and grass flying from his hooves, then bends into a wide turn before he reaches the far fence, before he can even see it. In the moment, feeling completely horse and sensing no need for greater completeness, he does not approach the limits to his freedom; he does not even allow them into view. The pasture is his kingdom, not his prison. In the moment, limits do not exist. In the moment, the world in all its sublime sufficiency belongs utterly to him. The sun shines for him as much as for any creature. The wind sings in his ear the best song it has ever sung. The water of the river tastes as it does, fresh and cold, to slake *his* thirst and please *his* tongue, as though there were no other.

Yes, I am making this up. Yes, of course, there is no way for me to know what passed through the mind of my horse. Except that Smokey was not invisible and I was not blind. Why, after a hard workout, would he celebrate his freedom by running still more? He felt good. He felt horse. He did not need to be told he would not feel that good forever, or indeed that he would not feel that good for long. The horse already knew something greater and more valuable. Deep in his bones he knew that if he felt this good, he should rejoice. He might even have known at some cellular level that if he felt this way today, he might feel this way again. Perhaps not tomorrow, nor the next day, but a creature that visits such exultation once surely believes in the chance he will exult again. This species of hope inhabits the body. It dwells in appetite, vigor, and possibility. Horses and other animals feel it and plainly show it. Perhaps it is the most important thing they teach us.

Many are the times I have walked into the woods dark of mind and stale in body. I have gone out *desperado*, shorn of hope, expecting nothing from the walk except the recapitulation of habit, merely going through the motions, trudging the ruts of behavior. But as often as not, something happens in the woods and I come back awakening to an opposite condition, which seems to have no name. Shall we call it *esperado*? Movement stirs breath, and together movement and breath stir appetite, which stokes the inborn spark of animation. Thus we kindle an animal hope.

Up across the hayfield, feeling the mild steepness of the slope, I return to the cabin. The weathered porch. The slam of the screen door. The domestic smell of enclosed space. The woodstove still warm from the morning fire. I have come back to the point of beginning. I have returned to the wooden desk, which is stained with a hint of green. I have returned to gaze out the window above the desk and to ponder land and sky. I am vexed once again by the buzzing of flies that have invaded this thick-walled sanctuary. The walk is over, yet the horse has not stopped running. I hear his hooves pounding the soft irrigated ground, as rhythmic as the beat of my own heart, as insistent as the click of keys as these words are typed. He runs, and as he runs, my griefs and dilemmas sweep into his wake.

Geranium

FROM THE SADDLE at the top of the Barn Arroyo I take a trail that bends away from the river. No more than a horse trail, it tunnels through a scrub of oaks and scrawny pines and soon meets a logging track. In one direction the track ties to the county road that joins El Valle to the rest of the world, and in the other it descends nearly to Arroyo Yerba Anís. Today I take neither option but cross the track and head downhill along a faint trail I cut years ago with the help of my son and daughter.

Past the first twenty paces, the trail did not need much cutting, for the forest opens into something nearly like the savannah it used to be. Only the initial thicket prevented easy passage. My children, then eight and twelve, chopped the brush and lopped the sapling branches that blocked the way. They worked with a joyful ferocity; each trimmed stem was a victory and deserved a victory shout. We hacked our way into the almost-savannah and then strolled through elegant, straight-trunked ponderosas to an upper reach of Arroyo Yerba Anís. Here the arroyo is shallow and easy to cross, on foot or horseback, although a storm-bent tree at the bottom forms a kind of arch under which riders must duck low. As the years passed, I favored this trail as a means to reach the ancient wagon trail between El Valle and Las Trampas, and the elk began to use it too, so that it wore a stripe into the land.

Many times, however, I veer away from the arroyo crossing and climb a knob that overlooks it, or would overlook it if you could see through the trees. The sides of the knob are overgrown with the usual tangle of distressed and stunted pines, but the top has a kind of ampleness. It is spacious but enclosed, like a well-proportioned room. Its floor is pine straw, its walls a loose palisade of pines and piñones, its ceiling a green vault of needles. Its furnishings consist of a moldering gray log that is wedded to the soil, some wisps of grass, and a scatter of bones.

Here you notice the foreleg of a horse, entire from scapula to hoof. And beyond it, a hind leg, equally complete, with the roots of tendons clinging to the joints and black lichen colonizing the grooves and planes of the bones where the last scraps of tissue once clung. On the far side of the log are sections of spine and a litter of ribs, the ends of which have been gnawed short by rabbits and rodents. The lower jaw, its two flat angles joined in a V, lies beside a stump. And at the center of this forest room, not far from where the living animal fell, lies the whitened skull. A small round hole, exactly the diameter of the tip of my little finger, marks the center of the forehead. If you were to draw lines from the root of each ear to the opposite eye, the hole would be at the center of the X. That is where you shoot a horse to kill it.

The bones belonged to Geranium, a gentle mare I bought for the children in 1988. She was already fifteen when I brought her home from a ranch on the east side of the mountains, together with a beautiful sorrel mare that I thought would make a saddle horse for me. I was wrong about the sorrel, which a few years later I sold back to the man I bought her from, but I was right about Geranium. She was dark bay with doelike eyes and a faint blaze in the center of her forehead. She was also friendly, imperturbable, and surefooted. I figured she would forgive the kids' mistakes and gradually teach them to ride. I was even surer about her when I learned she had once belonged to a friend. A decade earlier Lily Simpson had worked as the summer herder for the ranchers of the Bear Lakes Grazing Allotment, an expanse of bunchgrass parks and dark forest in the wild heart of the Pecos Wilderness. It surprised more than a few people that a group of leathery Hispanic cattlemen hired a slim, attractive gringa to tend their cattle in the high lonesome of the Sangre de Cristo range, but Lily did the job as well as anyone ever had, and Geranium was part of her string and did her job well too, as a saddle and packhorse, even standing up to a little roping. Lily knew Geranium as only a working partner could, and she said the mare, now getting on in years, would be ideal for kids. She also told me how the mare got her name: one morning, hoping to brighten her kitchen, she went out to buy a pot of geraniums. But the day had a logic of its own, and by afternoon Lily brought home a mare, and no flowers; she called the mare Geranium.

Most parents expect to pass to their children their love for the things they hold dear. The hunter teaches his son or daughter to hunt. The cook beguiles the children in the kitchen, who soon crave to measure and stir. But many parents learn that the opposite is no less common: the woodworker's child cannot abide sawdust but loves to swim. The painter's kid cannot draw but reads book after book. Children find their interests in their own way, and as time goes on those interests change, sometimes radically. A parent learns to adopt the child's interest as his own rather than insist on the reverse.

So it was in my family. Camping, horses, tending the farm, and other outdoor matters topped no one's list but my own. Not that Geranium was ignored. The children liked to pet her and feed her the alfalfa pellets we called horse cookies. But all through their elementary and high school years the farm was a less-than-favored destination, and it was a rare day that Katie, the firstborn, or David, four years her junior, urged me to fetch the saddle and set them up to ride. Still, there were occasions when everything seemed to mesh. I remember the bright spring day when Katie, who was then eight or nine, cantered

Geranium for the first time. She had been walking the mare down through the river pasture, across the stream, and in and out of the cottonwoods. On uphill pitches she kicked the mare into a trot, uphill trots being easier to sit than downhill ones. Now and again she rode up to the hayfield to check with me and show what she was doing.

I was prepping the field for irrigation, steering a utility vehicle in circles around the field and dragging two gangs of spike-tooth harrows to level the gopher mounds, break up manure, and aerate the soil. At two miles an hour in low-range four-wheel drive, it took a couple of hours to harrow the field, and I passed the time singing to the rock and roll that blared from the stereo.

Katie trotted to meet me near the middle of the field. "Daddy, I think I want to try a gallop. Is that okay?"

"Sure, but do it up here where the footing is good and I can watch you. Remember, the motion you want is to polish the saddle with your bottom."

Katie steered the mare toward a far fence and kicked her twice. Geranium broke into a trot. Katie kicked her again, and the mare rocked into an easy lope. Katie rocked with her, hair flowing, hands forward, back straight. Mare and child skimmed across the tawny, dormant grasses, and at the limit of the field they fish-hooked to a stop. Then Katie urged the mare again and came loping back. Katie beamed. She did not stop for congratulations but kept cantering in a wide arc, bending forward to coax the mare with her voice. Even atop a horse as small as

Geranium, Katie looked tiny, yet she rode with confident balance and a deep, secure seat.

She was circling the field a second time when her mother and brother appeared at the hayfield gate, coming up from the river. They walked hand in hand, the boy reaching high to hold onto his mother and stepping in the biggest strides he could manage across tussocks of grass. In her free hand Anne carried a pail of daisies that she and David had picked. She was even more beautiful than usual that day, her dark hair gleaming, her boy basking in her presence, awkward but resolute. She beamed and called out encouragement as Katie cantered past, while David, brow furrowed, eyed his sister and the hoof-pounding mare with gravity. Katie turned in the saddle, waved, and kicked the mare to keep her going. She kept her running to the far end of the field. The sun was drawing a warm mustiness from the harrowed field, jays cursed and other birds whistled from the trees, and the brightness of the day seemed to include no shadows.

But seasons come and go. Children grow. And the mare gets old.

Geranium had been a working horse. Her body bore the brunt of thousands of miles on rocky trails. Long days hunting lost cows. Heavy packs up and down mountain steeps. Over a lifetime a horse absorbs a lot of shocks in the knees of its forelegs. By the time Geranium reached twenty, her knees swelled with bony deposits, and even modest work gave her pain. A few years later the advancing arthritis had crippled her. In midsummer 1995, when David was almost ten, he and I rode on soft trails a mile and a half to an abandoned gravel pit where tadpoles abound in wet years and peepers sing from the edge of the woods. David rode Geranium, and I was on Spottie, a big white Arab loaned from a friend. We may have trotted a little on the outbound leg of the ride, but we didn't run.

Coming back, Geranium could hardly lift her right foreleg. She merely dragged her foot forward with every step, and she stumbled repeatedly, even at a walk. Clearly, this was her last day as a saddle horse, and David could sense it. She'd become dangerous for anyone to ride, and the pain she felt must have been severe. We shambled home silent and glum.

By autumn her condition had worsened. She limped badly even to graze on flat ground. I sought the advice of my neighbor, Lalo, a lifelong horseman. "I been wondering how long you gonna keep her," he said. "She don't look like she can make it through the winter." The vet said more or less the same. He outlined what a shot of bute or cortisone into her knee might do to deaden the pain but offered no encouragement. Then he said he could give me another kind of shot to put her down, but I would have to be careful to bury her lest the dope in her tissues poison scavengers too. That would take a backhoe. I said no thanks, shooting was cleaner, and the vet made sure I knew where to place the shot.

I put it off as long as I could, but by early December Geranium and I had run out of time. Winter cold was on us, and snow was soon to come. On the ninth I fetched her from the river pasture, walked her up to the corral, and fed her a big meal of grain. I left the gate open while she ate, and I walked down to sit by the river. Maybe I was hoping she would run. Coming back, I rehearsed all the arguments about her lameness, her age, and how poorly she was faring. I reviewed everything Lalo and the vet had said.

I was already wearing the gun in a shoulder holster beneath my jacket. Anne and the children were in town, forty miles away. I shut the dog in the house, grabbed a handful of alfalfa pellets from the shed, and returned to the corral. When I looked at Geranium, the blaze in the center of her forehead seemed uncommonly large and bright. I haltered her and led her to the barn where I'd hung a long soft rag on a crossbar. It was a flattened leg from a pair of sweatpants. Clean, soft cotton. Black. I stuffed it in a pocket of my jacket.

I led Geranium up the trail of the Barn Arroyo and into the forest toward Arroyo Yerba Anís, then angled toward the lonely knob with the spacious, open top that I'd checked out on a ride with Spottie weeks earlier. I picked up the big Arab's tracks as we climbed the knob — it had scarcely rained all fall, and they were still the only tracks there. I led Geranium past a pair of tall pines to the crown of the knob. Rare in the overgrown forest, the spot offered a bit of a view in one direction: you could look across the little valley of Arroyo Yerba Anís to the hills on the far side. Deep soft duff covered the forest floor. There was no sound. I stopped her. She faced slightly downhill. I gave her some horse cookies and fixed the black cloth over her eyes, tucking the ends under the straps of her halter. She didn't mind the blindfold, just nuzzled for more pellets. I gave her all I had. Then I drew the automatic, cocked it, and drew a bead on her blaze.

She kept moving her head, seeking my hand and more pellets. A few seconds passed, and when she held her head still for an instant, I fired.

It takes too long to say, "Her legs buckled." Never before or since have I seen anything fall the way she did. Before the sudden thunder of the gunshot reached its peak, she dove into the ground, striking hard on her muzzle, then rolled to her side. I turned away, holding the .45 at arm's length. I strode off a few steps, turned, saw her legs stretch out, rigid but twitching. Her body farted, and a river of blood gushed from her nostrils.

The blood flowed, gallons of it, like water from a bathtub tap. It flowed not for seconds but for minutes. The shot had smashed the wall of bone between the brain and the main airway. Now the flow of blood that had once fed her brain poured unimpeded out of the channel where she had drawn her breath. I lowered the hammer of the gun and ejected the clip. Then I unchambered the lone round still in it and put the bullet back in the clip. Blood still poured from her nostrils. I holstered the gun and crouched behind her, stroking her warm shoulder and saying, "I'm sorry, girl. I'm so sorry." Then I stood a few yards off and watched her. She twitched where I had patted her. I went back and patted her again.

I checked the entry wound. It was right in the blaze. I adjusted the blindfold, jarred by her fall, to cover her eyes again. I unclipped the lead rope and pulled it free from under her body. It was a relief to see that it was clean, bloodless. I would leave the halter on her.

The blood still poured from her muzzle. It ran into the duff and under it and a small red lake formed a few feet away, the blood rising up and topping the pine straw. I looked down. I was leaving bloody footprints. I must have stepped on blood-soaked duff. I said again, "I'm so sorry, girl," and stood a while watching her from the edge of the clearing. Finally, lead rope in hand, I headed back.

Geranium was a small horse, no more than fourteen hands. At most she weighed nine hundred pounds, but nine hundred pounds makes a lot of death, and Geranium's came loud and suddenly. The image is one of collapse, of a large mass falling, of all support and structure banished instantly and completely, as though they never existed. The concussion of the shot and the crash registered not so much through the ears as on the surfaces of the body: the face, the chest, the abdomen. A life went out; and then the jarred rough blocks of the world slammed back together, closing the space where the life had been. The clearing seemed to shake, as though tremulous.

And then the tremor, too, was gone. What remained was the forest, the indifferent trees towering above the cooling body of the mare.

The forest did not keep the body long. When I returned to the knoll two weeks later, the skeleton was already picked clean. I had not imagined the hunger of the forest to be so intense or so swift. Coyotes must have done most of the work, vultures having already migrated south, or perhaps a bear gorged on the carcass before heading to winter sleep. On a second visit a week later, I noticed that the tips of the short ribs had been gnawed away, and rabbit tracks dimpled the glaze of snow beside them. I had never thought of cottontails as scavengers, but here was proof. It seemed that every creature in the forest participated in Geranium's reduction and in the slow disassembly of her parts.

But something more than scavenging was going on. One day I visited the knoll, approaching through a thicket, not by the more usual route of the open path we used when I took her there. I lingered to note that the head and spine were now yards from where she'd first fallen and that a gristled leg had been dragged into oak brush. It was still winter, but a dry one, and no snow lay on the ground to record the tracks of visitors. I left by way of the usual path, which was a narrow alley through the scrub of young pines and shrubs that guarded the site. Where the scrub opened out, something lay in the center of the trail. Something white like a bone. Some piece of Geranium, I thought. But no, it was a skull, and I had just seen her skull. This was the skull of a cow.

Although I came to it from the wrong direction, there was no mistaking that the cow skull had been placed to lie at the entrance to Geranium's death site. It was a funerary marker, and it had not been there long.

I checked for tracks. Any creature bringing the skull would have crossed a patch of open ground devoid of duff, and the only tracks in the soft bare clay were ones I had made on visits when the cow skull was not present. Plus the lighter, less distinct tracks of coyotes and my own dog. In the years I had wandered this patch of forest, I had rarely encountered sign of another person this far back from both the river and the road, and never had I found such a sign in the depths of winter. I did not think a person had brought the skull to the entrance of the knoll. But I believed I knew the origin of the skull.

Some years earlier a cow had died—or a dead cow had been discarded—in the head of a gully beside a disused logging road a quarter mile away. The carcass appeared in summer, when food was abundant, and the forest community dawdled in consuming it. For months the gully reeked. In those days I rode the logging track regularly, and I would kick my horse and hold my breath as I passed by. Back then I also collected skulls, and I kept my eye on the cow's, but it vanished before it was clean enough to take home. Now perhaps this was that very skull, reappeared from a secret, inner space of the forest.

Tales that cast coyote as a trickster abound in native lore.

No other creature seems so instinctively inclined to mischief. Fox may be sly, but he is not bold enough for joking. Wolf is bold but not lighthearted. Bear is both bold and strong but too hazy-witted to deal in irony and symbolism. Cougar and bobcat, like all felines, are too self-absorbed. Among our cast of forest characters only raven also possesses the requisite curiosity and knack for mockery, but raven, being a bird, is too small for muscular pranks.

The business of the cow skull, however, was more than mischief. It was a judgment and a declaration. I have encountered only one other statement of similar heft and seriousness, and coyote unmistakably was its author. I stumbled upon this not-so-very cryptic message years ago in deep forest at the foot of a mountain that humans did not then and probably still do not frequent. Scrub oak blanketed the upper slopes of the mountain and made the area rich in acorns. And thick with bears. I had descended the oaky slopes and entered the forest, following a well-worn game trail. Where this trail met another that was also heavily trafficked there lay a bear skull, upside down, exactly in the center of the crossing. No other bones were close by; the skull had been brought there and conspicuously placed at a busy intersection. It was old and whitened, and the base of the cranium had long ago been opened and the brains eaten or rotted out. But the cranium was not empty. Bears no doubt think often, if fuzzily, about coyotes, and coyotes surely reflect even more upon the bears whose territories they share. In this instance a coyote that held strong views about its neighbors had deftly and accurately filled the cranium of the defunct bear with a compact mound of turds. The message was neither subtle nor hidden. It might have been a general statement about all bears or a more specific declaration about this particular bear, but in either case the author's point of view was clear.

The shat-in bear skull enlarged my idea of what a coyote might do, and as a result it did not seem a stretch to believe that a coyote might find, carry, and put down the skull of a cow to mark the death place of a horse. I believe that a coyote did this in the same way that I believe in small miracles and in the frequent intendedness of coincidence. Things happen in the forest that beggar belief, and we learn only of a few of those things, while explaining fewer still. If we attribute to coyote much of what seems strange to us, we are probably right enough, often enough, but no one can say if we are ever right completely. The forest resists exact understanding as much as the deepest dream. The roots of its mysteries reach into time and into the earth, as the roots of our dreams reach into the far, dark corners of our souls. When D. H. Lawrence, no stranger to dark corners, wanted to invoke the mystery of the soul, he summoned the image of the forest: "This is what I believe: That I am I. That my soul is a dark forest. That my known self will never be more than a little clearing in the forest. That gods, strange gods, come forth from the forest into the clearing of my known self, and then go back. That I must have the courage to let them come and go."

Lawrence's image of the soul is like the forest I think I

know. It is a place more often dark than light, a place where the half-light of dawn and dusk lasts longer than in other places. It is a place where creatures on strange errands trot through the gloom bearing odd burdens and odder messages that are rarely deciphered. It is a place where bones, memories, and myriad other things, some with names and some without, vanish and later reappear, only to vanish again like an unremembered dream. But in the forest, as in the soul, nothing is lost. Or so I believe. The things that seem lost are only hidden, and they may yet be seen again.

So it must be with the skull of the cow, which disappeared from the path to the knoll about three weeks after it was placed there. I looked for it then; I have looked for it since, but in the years since I shot Geranium I have never seen it again. The skull vanished as strangely as it had appeared, and when I noticed it was gone, the tracks in the mud and in the thin, crusty snow told me no more or less than they had before.

Not long ago, I visited the gully where the cow was left to rot. The white of her bones still peeks through the leaves and pine needles that carpet them. There is no skull, of course, only a half-hidden litter of vertebrae and ribs and the memory of an unremarkable and unpleasant death. There is nothing, in fact, to hold one's attention for long. A short walk farther and I stand at the edge of the forest on the crest of a low ridge over-looking the village *camposanto*, where other, better-known bones have come to rest. The graveyard is a garden of crosses and stones, where the remains of friends and respected elders lie trapped securely in the earth, beyond the reach of the animals and deities of the forest. Plastic flowers and tiny flags make the camposanto a brave little place, an outpost of care in an indifferent land. All the graves are aligned in parallel, feet to the road, and a fence of pig wire and cedar posts marks the boundary between the graveyard's respect for death and the chaos of the encroaching and more powerful forest. For the moment it is the forest that holds me, and I withdraw into the trees and follow the ridge upward, toward the crest of the hill that stands between the graveyard and my farm. As I go, the height of the forest diminishes, the trees growing smaller as the hill climbs toward its arid, sun-battered top.

The trees decline until the top is like a clearing. I approach it through contorted half-dead junipers and piñones, and then suddenly I am in the open, and I can see for miles. Above all, I can see the peaks. And that is the direction I look, for the peaks are stunning and always taller than I remember them. They claim one's attention the way a celebrity, shiny with charisma and reflected affection, claims the attention of a crowded room. Horses feel this too. They pay attention to long vistas. If Geranium were alive and I could ride her to this bald hilltop, she would heave and pant to catch her breath and then naturally turn to face the wide southeastern view out of which the peaks rise like an exclamation. I live with that view and seek it the way I seek the companionship of friends. Although I can see the peaks from down at the cabin and in the fields, on the hilltop the feeling of the vista is different. Partly, this is because the elevation of the hill places more of the mountains in view. But the forest also has an influence. The sight of the high peaks seems to gain power when I have been among the big trees a while. Breaking out to the hilltop clearing, I am like a swimmer who has come up for air. I rise from a world of shadow and mystery, a world of hazy allurements and unintelligible possibilities, and suddenly, lifted by the swell of the hill, I enter the clarity of the sky.

From the hilltop, I see the valley below the peaks, its tidy fields, and the serpentine arroyos, clogged with brush, that run between the fields. I see the red-roofed church, tiny in the distance, and the scattered houses and barns and the wind-ruffled cottonwoods along the river. I see the shaggy hills that enfold the valley and the dark canyons that cut between them. The hills are green in the near distance and then grow bluer, mile by mile, as they stretch away and rise into mighty ridges, yielding finally to the stony volumes of the peaks.

The rest of the land is land; the peaks are sculpture. Everything about them pleases the eye: the paths of their avalanche chutes and the contours of their shadowed cirques, the scree slopes, the tundra ridges, the sprawl of their raw rock faces. They gladden the heart winter and summer, no matter if they dazzle with snow or show the impassive gray of their billion-year-old bones. And in all seasons, in all lights from dawn to dusk and under the glow of moon and stars, one thing is immutable: the horizon line of those peaks against the sky. It is changeless and lies engraved, permanent and exact, upon the crust of the earth and, no less, upon the hardest plates of memory. It is a sacred line, holy like an altar. People who live amid mountains carry such lines in their hearts because it is what they see when they lift their eyes to the hills, as the psalmist did, *whence cometh my strength.*

Some feelings resist expression for years or decades. Some never submit. The sight of the peaks has long struck me as a kind of a prayer I am supposed to know but cannot find the words to. They are like the chorus of a hymn I want to sing but cannot finish: *the mountains rise like, the mountains rise like* . . . but what is it that they rise like, *to the sky?*

I stand in the clearing and trace anew the outline of the peaks against the radiant New Mexico sky, and I wonder, if I were blindfolded, could I draw the sacred line of that horizon on paper? I think I could, if only I had a hand for drawing, and I close my eyes and visualize the line as though I might burn it with memory, left to right, on the inside of my eyelids. First, on the left, stands the rounded top of Trampas Peak, and then the amputated V where the chasm of the Río de las Trampas hides behind blue hills. Next comes the sharp inverted cone of Jicarilla Peak, which subsides to a knife-blade ridge that runs flat and straight until it meets the jagged crags of Sheepshead. And Sheepshead, in spite of its homely name, soars like the Matterhorn to sharp-pointed heights. After Sheepshead comes the great rounded fin of North Truchas, followed by the swollen pyramid of Middle Truchas, and peeking over the shoulder of the middle sister, the pointed finial of South Truchas, which scrapes the sky at 13,103 feet, the tallest mountain but one in the region. The sacred line of these peaks, seen from this valley, is replicated nowhere else on earth. It is the signature of this mountain range, of this place, and of this valley, and it is written on the deed of my soul.

And then, eyes newly opened, an idea comes to me. I think I have the answer to the chorus of the hymn that has been escaping me. I think maybe I am beginning to hear the whole song. The mountains rise not like a thing, but like the spirit behind things, or like spiritedness itself. They rise like meaning. They rise with purpose and clarity. They rise like a promise of understanding in an ambiguous and paradoxical world. They rise not like hope itself, but like the promise that something as grand as hope might exist. The mountains rise like meaning to the sky.

The idea is a kind of nourishment. I stand there feeding on it. When I am full, I take a last grateful look at the peaks. Then I turn to go, facing the forest anew. I descend into the dark wood, a diver returning to the depths. The green shade of the trees quickly envelops me. I resume my walk, off-trail, destination unknown, looking for I don't know what, but the feeling of the walk is different now because the peaks are with me. They anchor the edges of the world, and they guarantee a limit to the drift and strangeness of things. They are behind me and available, if I need to see them, and they rise like meaning to the sky.

One day I will be walking in the forest far from the knoll where I shot Geranium and I will come across a bone. Let us say that the bone will belong to Geranium, but I will have no way of knowing. When I pick it up and brush off the shreds of leaf and clots of dirt that cling to it, I will be unaware that the bone once belonged to the mare that stood just outside the circle of my family. Perhaps the bone will show decay, but perhaps not. In our dry climate bones retain their exquisite architecture for decades. If it is a vertebra, I will marvel at the winglike structures that anchored the muscles of the back. I will admire the roundness of the channel that housed the spinal cord and the delicacy of the apertures through which nerve fibers and fluids passed. I will consider the rugged surfaces where cartilage nested to receive the neighbor vertebrae, and I will feel awe for the grace and sturdiness of the entire design, which was a small but vital component of a creature that was born to fly across the land, distilling poetry from speed. Never knowing whether the bone is Geranium's, I will nevertheless think of Geranium, for I was fond of her for many years and the act of killing her left its mark on my heart. Or I will recall other horses or animals to which the bone might have belonged, or, unfastening myself from literal associations, I will recall the past in more general terms, welcoming, I hope, the memories of loved ones and friends, and the relationships that bound me to them, those who died or tore away in violence or simply drifted off, the bones of whose memory lie scattered in the forest of my soul in patterns and locations I will never understand. No matter if the recollection is one of pain and grief or of fond happiness, I will hope to have the courage to let the recollection come into me, as into a clearing, and to appreciate it in the fullness of its exquisite detail, and then to let it go, receding anew into the dimness of the forest, perhaps never to be seen or felt again.

Paradiso

In January one year, a bear ransacked the cabin site. The doors and windows held, but the bear threw the benches off the porch, overturned the table under the cottonwood tree, and jackstrawed the chairs. He tore the horse skull off the shed wall and scattered chunks of firewood, spools of wire, and a bundle's worth of metal fence posts with the violence of a tornado. It was admirable, in a way. A human drunk can achieve high levels of disorder, but somewhere deep in the occlusion of his mind a scrap of brain will still twitch with intention, like a voice in a cavern whispering "I'll show them," or even "Destroy." The sour bear surpasses that. There is no voice, no intention at all. The randomness attains a kind of perfection, like the chaos of the big bang. And so you find the skull under the upended table but atop the dish soap. The chair is inexplicably woven into the fence. The outdoor sink has toppled from its stand, yet the kindling is neatly in it.

You conclude that the bear had serious complaints. It was enraged at creation. It wanted to hibernate but couldn't. It was hungry, but there was no food. And so it protested the performance of the world, which from an ursine point of view was completely unacceptable. It was easy to have sympathy for the bear, because that winter the world was performing pretty badly from a human point of view too. Snowless January was behaving like April. It was far too warm, which made it bad for bears, and far too dry, which made it bad for nearly everyone and everything else. Everyone in the village knew we were in for a dry year, but maybe the bear in its inchoate way knew more. As it turned out, we were headed into the jaws of a record-breaking, mummifying drought.

In February, when the peaks should have gleamed with snow, they were pitifully bald big rocks. Skiers in Santa Fe and Taos mourned. Farmers and ranchers bit their nails. "Wait a bit," they said. "The snows of March can bail us out. They're most often the deepest of the year." But then March came, and snow didn't. For me personally the month could hardly have started worse. My closest friend was in the Santa Fe ICU. Days earlier he'd risen from his bed in the small hours of the night and was heard to say, "I don't feel so good." Then an artery in his brain burst, and he sagged to the floor. On the first of

March the nurses disconnected the machines, and the people who transplant organs went to work.

It didn't snow or rain in April either, not enough to measure. It was my habit to visit Lalo every week or two, and so I called on him one cloudy April day. His father and mother had been like grandparents to me when I first came to the village. We'd known each other for almost thirty years and had been friends for close to twenty. Even into his late seventies he still worked like a bull, irrigating, haying, and tending cattle, but now at eighty-one he slept tethered to an oxygen tank, and his breath whistled and rasped. We took care of a piece of land on the far side of the river together. Its ownership was split; my neighbor Alex and I owned half and the other owners, all absentee, appointed Lalo to represent their interest and make use of it as he saw fit. But this year, Lalo said, he would not try to do much over there. He didn't feel up to it. Oh, and he had some news about his health. The trouble with his breathing wasn't just emphysema anymore: "The doctors say there is cancer in my lungs."

He looked me hard in the eyes to gauge my reaction, and I must have looked as blank as a sheet of white paper. All I could do was swallow and nod. I could not think of anything to say that did not sound trite, even before I said it. The news was a shock, but it was also expected. A new grayness had seeped into the lines of Lalo's face, and there was a hint of defeat in the way he shuffled between the stove and the kitchen table. He hadn't felt genuinely well in a couple of years, and now he'd received the heavy sentence he and everybody close to him had thought was probably coming. Feeling stupid, I finally said something about how sorry I was, and then I felt stupider. With the sense that I was stumbling through the steps of an awkward dance, I asked what his doctors had said about treatment. Lalo spread his broad, weathered hands palms-down on the table and stared at them as though they belonged to someone else. "They want me to take some chemo, so I will. We just gonna see what happens," he said. "I got no other choice."

Lalo — short for Olivario — Romero was the last of several generations of village men who "followed the sheeps." At the age of fourteen in the early years of the Great Depression, he left home to tend camp for his father, Jacobo, who also herded sheep from a tender age. I can't remember if his first trip was to Colorado or Wyoming, but wherever it was, the country was hard and far from home, and no one, least of all his father, worried whether Lalo liked what he was doing. Work being work, Lalo's only choice was to work, and he never again darkened the door of a school. A few years later when he was eighteen, Lalo joined the Civilian Conservation Corps and was assigned to a camp near El Rito, New Mexico, which lay forty or fifty miles west of El Valle across many a steep-walled canyon and the Río Grande itself. What sheepherding had not toughened, the CCC did. Lalo worked heavy labor with pick, shovel, and axe and fended for himself in the all-male rough-and-tumble of the camp. Most of his wages went home to his mother and family. He said he liked it, although once in a while he got lonely for home. The homesickness got so bad one time, he just faced east and started walking. There was no particular road or trail to follow, and until he crossed the Río Grande the natural drainages of the country between him and home ran mainly north and south. No matter. He just kept walking. Up one rugged ridge, down the other side, one after another. The way he told the story, he wanted to see his mother and eat a home-cooked meal pretty badly, so he walked all of one day, and the night that followed, and all of the day after that. He said it was not that big a deal; he got home fine, saw his mother, and ate some decent food. The only trouble was that he had worn out his government-issued shoes and he couldn't get another pair.

Lalo turned twenty the year the Japanese bombed Pearl Harbor. He served in the Pacific as a medic, an experience he declined to speak of in his later years. When the war ended, he came back to sheepherding, and to beer. His routine seldom varied. He spent spring, summer, and fall in Wyoming, where he did not drink, and winters in El Valle, where he did. On the range he was sober, conscientious, and dependable. He worked for one company for over twenty years. Back in El Valle he inhabited a beery haze. I first met him in 1975. He was the most inoffensive, genial drunk I'd ever known. He would pass an entire January day leaning against the bed of his tan pickup, oblivious to the cold, chatting with whomever came by, chain-smoking cigarettes that he could roll even when he could not stand, and working his way through a case of beer. One by one he'd drop the empties into the bed of the truck, where they'd join the empties of days before and clatter all together when he drove to Peñasco for a fresh case. If I passed by, I would stop and say hello. He would greet me, or anyone, with a handshake and a lunatic grin, and energetically launch into a serpentine run-on sentence that lasted minutes and never gave a hint of destination. He spoke half in English, half in Spanish, with the words mashed together and no pauses for punctuation. Some people seemed to understand him, but I never made sense of what he said. Fortunately, my incomprehension did not bother him. We'd pantomime our way through the semblance of a conversation, and then I'd continue on my way, knowing no more than when I'd said hello. Lalo baffled me in those years, and the person behind the beer, if there was a person, remained a mystery. Then each spring, like a wild goose, the mystery departed for the north.

In the fall of 1978, in Wyoming, things changed. Lalo was somewhere in the backcountry along the western Colorado and Wyoming border with two thousand sheep. His camp tender had taken the wagon to fetch supplies, and Lalo did not expect to see him for several days. Lalo rode out one morning, as he rode out every morning, to check on the sheep. The spare horse, which was loose, trailed along. But it was acting odd. Before the morning was far advanced—and details were soon lost to amnesia—some pulse of equine pique or insanity caused the horse to attack Lalo's saddle horse. It ran in, spun, and launched a kick. The saddle horse dodged, and the shod hoof caught Lalo full on the lower leg, splintering the bones. Lalo managed to slide to the ground, and there he stayed. The fractures would not allow him to move. Soon he passed out, and not much later it began to rain. He lay in the cold and wet for two days, hypothermic and in shock. Fortunately his saddle horse stayed close, which was the miracle that saved him. When a herder from another outfit rode near, the horse whinnied. The herder came over to investigate the loose but still saddled horse, and he found Lalo.

After that, Lalo showed an iron will. He never drank another beer, and he gave up cigarettes too. I recall that after his leg healed he went back for one more season in Wyoming, maybe two, but soon he retired from the "sheeps" and stayed year-round in El Valle, where he took full charge of the family farm, relieving his aging father, whom he seemed, in the remarkable coherence of his new habits, more and more to resemble. He had remained a bachelor all his life, although in the decades I knew him he had a steady companion who kept her own house in a nearby village, and he loved company, welcomed visitors, and always had time to spare for friends. As he eased through his sixties and into his seventies, he seemed to take ever-greater pleasure in the modest distractions of the valley: the companionship of neighbors, the rescue and nursing of a dogied calf, the fidelity of a good dog. Even when no one else did, he stayed out of the feuds that periodically wrapped themselves around the village like a strangler vine, and he cared for his parents and his land with unremitting diligence. His father passed away in 1985 and his mother a decade later. As the years wore on, the motley stream of relatives, neighbors, travelers, and friends of friends who had sat with his parents under the deep portal of the Romero house or in its warm kitchen now came to sit with him. Everyone called him friend.

The announcement of his cancer seemed to shock Lalo least of anyone. It was more like a presence, long in the room, that had finally received its name. When I said something hopeful about the coming chemotherapy, Lalo shrugged as though to show he was not interested in the construction of optimism. I asked him to let me help with the farm. "Don't worry about the land across the river," I offered. "I'll irrigate it, yours and mine."

"Okay. Thanks," he said, as though the offer meant something. But in practical terms, it did not. In that year, which surpassed even the worst years of the 1950s, irrigation all but ceased. In the winter there was no snow, and when summer came, there was no water.

I seem to forget in the winter and relearn every spring that the payoff of irrigation is not harvest. It is first water.

In a normal year the task arrives in April when the trees are bare and the village farms, still in the grasp of cold nights, are drained of color. August's hay-cutting and the autumn foraging of cattle and horses barbered the fields roughly. Then winter snow mattes down the scruff that remains. By April the fields have the frowsy look of a head too long on the pillow. But the days soon lengthen at a gallop, and the soil warms by tiny increments, summoning waxy buds from the branches of the cottonwoods.

It is evening when I go to the ditch to turn out the water for the first irrigation of the year. In another endeavor a bell might ring or a horn blow to mark such a beginning, but this job is solitary and quiet, although I am not really alone. The valley is alive with piping and twittering. The sounds come from every nook of habitat: the river trees, the arroyo brush, the pines and junipers of the dry hills. From a perch in one of the cedars that line the ditch, a shrieking robin, fluent and inane, screams its single question and answers it, over and over without pause. In the shadows below, the ditch water hurries down its channel, a dark, aortic flow. For the next twenty-four hours the water is mine to use.

Aside from the rare potsherd or obsidian point, the acequia, or irrigation ditch, is probably the oldest artifact of human occupation in the valley. It predates the oldest buildings, and it has outlived what has been hewn or hacked into the trees. The word itself, drawn from an Arabic root, ties this place to Africa. The Moors were masters of irrigation, and they took their skills to Iberia and married them to the life already there, along with chess, algebra, and their graceful architecture.

The acequia begins a mile and a half up the valley at a structure that diverts a portion of the river's flow into the acequia's mouth. The structure is called a dam — *una presa* — but it is not so much a barrier as a ledge (now of concrete, formerly of cribbed logs) that essentially armors a headcut in the river and prevents it from moving upstream. Without the presa the river would long ago have deepened its channel past the reach of the ditch's mouth. The river leaps over the ledge of the presa and tumbles loudly fifteen or twenty feet into a bed of boulders. From there it courses down the bottom of the valley. The acequia, meanwhile, veers quietly to the side, bound for houses and fields. It falls, obedient to gravity, but barely, almost imperceptibly so, and there are places where you would swear, if you didn't know better, that its gradient was as dead flat as a contour line. It flows calmly along a route that encloses as much of the deep-soiled valley as the necessity of maintaining flow will allow it to embrace. The trick of the ditch is to flow not so slowly that it clogs with silt or pools and tops its banks nor so fast that it drops past land that it otherwise might water. It makes its circuit of the lower valley evenly and cleanly and with enough downward pitch to maintain a forceful current. At my farm, which is the last before the canyon, the current of the ditch increases. Steep hills crowd in and close the valley off, forcing the acequia, once it has rimmed the upper limit of my hayfield, to take a hard downhill turn and hurry back to the river.

I look forward to the water in April. The ditch is nearly always calf-deep with snowmelt. Owing to its flat bottom and even sides, the voice of the water is low and steady, like the warning growl of a dog. It makes a simple assertion, not an argument. It demands the respect of being handled right.

The acequia serves the field by means of five water gates, or *compuertas*, that divert ditch flow into the mouth of a subsidiary ditch, called a *regadera*, which in turn carries water to the field. The compuertas are frames that allow a wide board to be inserted across the flow of the ditch, forcing water to spill through a trap on the side. Each of the compuertas has a different character. The oldest is hidden in a tunnel of junipers and consists of an ancient hollowed log, deeply buried athwart the ditch. Like the presa, it functions as a ledge and props the water of the ditch where it can be got out through the trap. All that is needed is to drop a water-smoothed board into the slots fixed into the hollowed part of the log. Two other compuertas lie in full sun amid a tangle of willows, close to each other but facing different directions, like twins focused on separate tasks. Another is in disrepair, undercut by erosion so that the log that undergirds it cants the wrong way, and it must be dammed to double the normal depth to force out a useful flow of water.

I go to the one that is brightest and noisiest—bright because it is located where the ditch clings to a steep bank and the water tumbles out from it frothy and white, and noisy because the falling water drums on what was once the ramp of a stock trailer, which is rigged with posts and wire to shield the bank from eroding. From the ramp the water spills into a short channel of cobbles through which it surges to the field. I step into the ditch, careful of the footing and hoping my rubber boots, after a winter of storage, have not sprung a leak. I remove the wooden slot that blocks the trap. Its handle is a length of chain anchored at either end by fence staples. I lay the slot on the sandbags that guard the edge of the ditch and pull a grayed plywood plank from the leaves where it has lain all winter. In the summer garter snakes hide from the sun under such boards, but April weather is still too cold for them to have emerged. I place the board against the restraints of the compuerta so that it dams the ditch. Water churns and backs against the board and bursts through the side outlet, carrying with it a small shower of gravel that clatters onto the ramp. I turn upstream and shovel more sand and gravel from the ditch bottom and throw it against the base of the board to seal gaps through which long feathers of water shoot. Each shovelful cancels more of the hiss of escaping water and sends a new clatter of tiny stones onto the ramp. The voice of the water rises, arguing with the board. The water backs and pools against the barrier, and as it deepens I feel it compress my boots against my calves. Soon the gate reaches capacity and a luminous curtain of water spills over the board, resuming its journey down the acequia to the next gate, where it will be put to use. But most of the ditch's flow now gushes through the outlet of the compuerta. It tumbles onto the ramp and then into the cobbled channel, where it rushes to the field babbling like children released from school.

The formal name of the ditch is long and winding like the ditch itself — *la acequia abajo del valle de San Miguel* — but we only ever call it acequia abajo, the lower ditch. It is one of three principal ditches in the village. The *acequia arriba* and the *acequia del llano* are its siblings. On the acequia abajo there are seventeen water rights, or *surcos*, held by fifteen *parcientes* including me. I handle one surco, which entitles me to irrigate for twenty-four hours at a time in rotation with the other parcientes. Under our customary rules, that means I get the water at six in the evening and give it up at six the next day. If the water in the ditch is ample, and it usually is, then twenty-four hours is enough time to give all of the land served by the ditch a good, deep drink. And getting the water at six in the evening means that in April or early May when I turn out the water for the first irrigation of the year, the evening sun is already low and its light soon comes red and flat out of the west.

When I first learned to irrigate, I would start working the water the instant it touched my field. My teacher was Lalo's father. Jacobo did not give instruction so much as do as he would normally do, and his student could observe and do likewise or flail away on his own. I was in a hurry to show what a hard worker I was and flailed more than I knew, attacking the hard ground too soon. Now I wait as water gurgles down the length of the regadera, pushing the inevitable raft of leaves and dead grass before it. It is good to let the water soak and soften the soil before trying to dig. It is good to lean on your shovel, gloved and hatted against the spring chill, and listen to the mutter of the water and the periodic squawks of robins. As the water spills from the regadera and spreads down the slope of the field, I begin to hear something more, something midway between the fizz of carbonation and the purr of a cat. It is the sound of the ground drinking, releasing minute bubbles from between its grains of loam, and the bubbles pop with the murmur of a thousand sips, a chorus of delicate kisses.

The task of irrigation, when I finally set about it, is to apportion water among the regadera and its capillaries so that they carry water across the roll of the land to every patch of sod served by the compuerta. I use the shovel to open gaps in the side of the regadera so that water spills out in a volume sized to the amount of land the flow must cover. The idea is to create a smooth sheet of water that creeps steadily down the slope of the field, with no need for further adjustment, giving every plant of alfalfa or timothy a deep long drink and reaching the limit of its run more or less simultaneously all along its breadth. That is the ideal, and achieving it is probably rarer than hitting a hole-in-one or pitching a no-hitter. I wouldn't know for sure; I have never witnessed such a thing.

I go about my work, chopping notches in the regadera through which the water runs and shoveling out rafts of leaves and dead grass that impede the flow. Where the trampling of animals or the growth of vegetation has compressed the regadera, I dig it wider and deeper. All the while, I listen for the hollow-sounding gurgle of water swirling down a drain. My field is beloved by gophers, and their holes are everywhere. The holes drain off the water and leave the downslope sod as dry as jerky. When I find a hole, I dig up the earth around its mouth and stamp the loose earth into the hole to stopper it.

The dog brings me a stick to throw, which after only a few fetches is gummily coated with drool. Inevitably he drops it in a swirl of muddy water, which makes the prospect of picking it up even more repellent than usual. This dog, a border collie like other dogs I've had, has never learned his predecessors' trick of moving downhill from where I irrigate and waiting for gophers to stagger from their flooded tunnels. Those collies would snatch the sodden rodents from the doors of their burrows, molar them briefly to stop their wiggling, and swallow them whole. This collie thinks only about sticks.

I dig and chop; I try to tune the regadera, releasing more water here, less there. I throw the repulsive stick. I stamp shut another gopher hole. And another. The first irrigation of the year always demands more work than any other. A winter's worth of debris has accumulated in the regaderas, and the gophers have had free rein for too long. Tractors, the hooves of animals, and the frost heaving of winter have deformed the ditches, and the soil is dry from spring winds and slow to take its drink. Nearly an hour passes. The work is warm. I have taken off my jacket and thrown it to the high side of the regadera. Only a little light is left in the day. The set of the water is imperfect, but it is always imperfect. Maybe better next time. I stop and look down the length of the field. While my back was turned, a sheet of water has spread across the field. It glimmers now. It glimmers as it never will again this year, for the grass, as it grows taller, will perforate and obscure it. The sheen of the water captures the blue of the sky, and the sudden red daggers of sunset streak across it. Robins, careful of the dog, swoop down to probe the damp ground. They call to each other, high-pitched and strident. The ground hisses with the sound of drinking, and I hear myself speaking to it — or maybe I only think the words. But what I am saying I have said every year: "Drink. Drink and wake up. Time to begin again. Drink, and we start over, you and me."

All but the top of the sun has dropped behind the ridgeline. The blue of the sky has dulled, and the sheen of water, now spread across an acre of spring grass, is silver with reflection. It captures the sky in its mirror so that the sky seems to lie on the field, heaven and earth united, but the mirror quivers with the water moving in it, like the hide of an impatient beast.

The moment slowly shifts. The shadow of the ridge spreads across the field and dims the water's sheen, but the cloudless sky remains suffused with light. It is the kind of light you see in the paintings of American luminists. It imbues the things it touches with a kind of purity that holds the darkness of the world at bay. It causes time to pause, and the living things that pause with it hold their breath. Such a light now shimmered on the watered field, and the sight of its pewter sheen, in the still-ness of approaching night, was proof yet again that the payoff of irrigation, far more than harvest, is first water.

I never asked Lalo if he saw things that way. I just assumed he did. For years he irrigated a field next to mine and I would see him there, leaning on his shovel, hands on the end of the handle, chin on his hands, looking at the spreading water. If you spend much time in irrigated country, you see a lot of people strike that posture, and it is not hard to imagine part of what passes through their minds. My friend Palemon confirmed that for me when we were traveling together late one night. Palemon and I were friends but also sometimes adversaries. For a half dozen years we served on committees and boards together, enmeshed in more meetings and negotiations than either of us would have liked, and we did not always see eye to eye. We were familiar but not close, friendly but wary, never opening enough to show much to the other. But there were moments of exception, and one came as we drove home from a long and moving meeting with leaders of a nearby pueblo.

Palemon's roots in northern New Mexico go as deep as non-Indian roots can go. I imagine that I hear the ancient bond of place in the old-time sound of his name: *pah-ley-món*. He was a trusted elder in the farm and ranch community, and it was easy to see why. He was thoughtful, practical, patient, and judicious. Also sly and tough, when he needed to be. He cut a good figure too. I remember, on the night of our meeting with the tribe, how he looked in the dark cab of the truck. It was just the two of us, and I was driving. He sat in the passenger seat erect but at ease. I sensed that he was mulling what the tribe had told us, and what we'd said back, and his thoughts seemed to satisfy him. He looked contented and self-contained, and the dash lights cast off just enough glow to highlight the dignity of his features: the Spanish nose, the strong chin, the dark brows. Stealing glances from the road ahead, I looked at him and thought, "That profile belongs on a coin."

Our meeting with the pueblo lasted from the late hours of a summer's afternoon into the pitch darkness of night. It was a dinner and a talk, and our guests did the talking. The issue was access to sacred sites. For three-quarters of a century the successive owners of a large tract of private land had restricted or refused the tribe access to some of its holiest places. Now the ownership of the land had changed, and together with others, Palemon and I, as members of a board charged with tending the land, were in a position to be helpful. The gathering involved nine or ten of us who were developing new arrangements for the property, together with a delegation of equal size from the pueblo. Among the pueblo delegation was the tribe's cacique, its oldest and highest religious leader, whose presence underscored the profundity of the occasion.

We met in a large room, cavernous and dim, and as dinner was cleared away one of the tribe's leaders rose to make a presentation. He spoke in English of the history of his people, how they had come to the region centuries ago, how signs had been revealed to them in these particular mountains that this was the place for them to sink their roots, and how forever afterward they had built their village now here, now there, but always close to the land to which they now petitioned for renewed access. Their religion was not separate from the land but part of it, as one's sense of hearing or sight is part of one's experience of life, and because they could not practice their religion in full without engaging all of their religious senses, they needed access to the places to which the religion was tied. The speaker added that their relationship to the land did not solely concern what they needed from the land, for they believed the land needed them as well. Without their rituals and prayers, he said, the land itself would suffer.

For generations members of the tribe had been compelled to request that the owners of the property allow their visits. Some requests were granted, but many were not. Sometimes the request was not made because its denial was certain. Sometimes it was not made because it was insulting to have to make it. Often the people had to acquiesce to the denial of access; other times they smuggled themselves in and out. No matter the outcome, said the speaker, the situation was intolerable, and it must not continue. In a better world, the land would belong to the pueblo, and the humiliating question of asking permission to visit it would never arise. He closed with these words: "We were here for centuries before your earliest ancestors arrived, and we will be here for as many centuries more as time contains. We are not going anywhere." And then he asked for questions.

The questions that came were innocent and pragmatic: Do you need access to all of the property or only to some of it? Would your visits involve a lot of people? Would they involve killing or collecting things, like game animals or plants?

The answers consisted mainly of variations on the theme

"that depends." But to arrive at such a thrifty, albeit slightly evasive response, the pueblo delegation spoke heatedly among themselves for five, ten, fifteen minutes, or more. The process was repeated for each question. All but the cacique spoke, and they spoke in their own language, without translation. They spoke with emphasis and energy and, judging from the tone and cadence of their speeches, with considerable oratorical skill. They seemed at times to disagree, but each speaker was fully and patiently heard, sometimes interrupted by choruses of "Naunh, naunh," as the others offered their assent: "That is true." "It is so."

As the discussions wore on, I was interested to observe one young man with whom I had a friendly if slight acquaintance. I knew him mainly as a laborer and general handyman, but several people had troubled to tell me — always in awed tones — that this young man was "studying" to be a religious leader, that he was embarked on a rare and demanding path. Now came proof, of a sort. He spoke more often and more vigorously as the debates wore on. Unlike the others, he rose to his feet when he spoke, and although he was the youngest person in the room there was no shyness in his manner. He brimmed with conviction. It seemed to me the other speakers increasingly deferred to him, and I marveled at the reversal of his status, from day to night, from laborer to leader, from youthful adult to someone who might trump his elders on matters of gravity and import. He seemed to embody a kind of parable about identity in northern New Mexico, or about identity generally — that what you first see is often less than what is there, that the standard measurements of status and position seldom tell more than a sliver of the truth.

The dialogue passed its crescendo and began to wind down. The questions, together with the long-debated answers, came to an end. It was time for the board to respond, and our reply seemed to surprise some of the tribal leaders: yes, we said, things will now change; we will need to work closely together so that the tribe's activities do not conflict with other uses of the land, but "You do not have to ask permission anymore." At this, the aged cacique, who had watched and listened, saying little, raised his head, and something like a smile split his stony face. In a little while, speaking for the tribal delegation, he bid us thank you and good night.

A little later, Palemon and I took the dark road home. We had much to ponder. If we had impressed the Indians a little by our readiness to support their needs, they had impressed us even more. Over the years both of us had heard many speeches and arguments by Native Americans about the sacredness of land and water. Most were sincere; some plainly were not. But the majority fell into a pattern that seemed rehearsed and even obligatory, like a candidate's stump speech. We agreed that what we had heard this night was something deeper and more soulful, and we talked about the practicalities of the pueblo's needs, and about the demands that other pueblos would bring forward, and the possible resentment of non-Indians that the tribes were getting special treatment.

"Other groups will say that the land is sacred to them too," I ventured.

"And they will be right," said Palemon. There were different ways to have feeling about the land, he said, different kinds and levels of connection. Some were shaped by tradition, some by an individual's experience. But, he said, "the feeling doesn't have to be religious to be sacred."

We had come now to a busy stretch of road, and the glare of headlights and road signs flashed through the cab. Palemon looked relaxed and fresh, although the hour was late.

"What about you, Palemon? Are there places on the land that feel sacred to you?"

Palemon fell silent. The only sound was the thrum of the truck barreling down the road. I worried that I had asked too personal a question and that he was searching for a polite way of telling me so. But then he spoke.

"There are places where I take my cattle—up on the Valle Vidal, for instance—that are very special to me. I guess you could call them sacred. And other places I knew as a child, where I played or herded. But you know, I was thinking, it's not just places but certain acts, things you do, that have the feeling of being sacred, the feeling of almost being in church."

"Like what?"

"Well, there is a certain moment I look forward to in the year. It comes in the spring, and it comes when the field is ready and the acequia is running and you open the gate. It is when you put the first water on the field."

Now Palemon stole a glance at me, to check my response. I nodded, and he went on, "I don't know why, but it always seems peaceful at that time. You can hear the water spreading across the ground, and you can see it sort of shining, and the time seems separate and different from the other times I irrigate or work that field. It is the time, you know, of a beginning. You are starting over again. It is like a birth."

We were coming into town now, and the reflected yellow of streetlamps bathed the inside of the truck. Palemon had crossed his arms in front of him, and he no longer sat erect but leaned comfortably against the door. He was smiling. "I love that time," he said. "I love when it is time for the first water."

In the dry year when Lalo was diagnosed with cancer my chance to deliver first water to the hayfield came later than usual. Because of upstream construction, the *mayordomo* did not begin the rotations until early May. At last he called to tell me when my turn would come. On the appointed day I waited long past six for the water to arrive, but the flow in the ditch was only a few inches deep, less than a third of a normal surco. Probably someone had left a gate open, and the water that was due to me was running into the wrong field. I called the mayordomo and talked to neighbors; I checked up and down the ditch for compuertas left open, where water might be spilling out. But there were no gates open, and the entire content of the river was flowing into the mouth of the acequia. (Springs brought the river feebly back to life not far downstream.) The trickle that reached me a mile and a half below was all the water there was. The dry ditch had swallowed the rest.

I spread the water among a half dozen cuts of a single regadera, and the water, set loose upon the sod, scarcely moved. It took an hour to advance a dozen yards. The volume of water was too puny and the thirst of the parched ground too great. The leading edge of the water did not flow so much as seep, and I stared as it crept slowly forward, darkening the cracked soil, fissure by fissure and grain by grain. At such a rate, not half the field would get a drink in the allotted time of twenty-four hours. This year there would be no sunset gleam on a sheen of water, no gurgle of the ditch nor chorus of sipping from the ground, no call to new beginnings. There would be instead only the fall of night and a sense of futility and impending loss. Not just Lalo was sick. The land was, the valley was. And there was no prospect of improvement. The mountains, bereft of snow, had no runoff to offer, and significant rain was unlikely before July. Maybe I'd be able to keep the top edge of the field watered and green, but the rest would simply burn.

No one that summer expected to make a crop of hay or of anything else. Lalo liked to say that the mark of a good year was to look up at the peaks on Fourth of July and see patches of snow. This year we looked to the mountains in May, and all we saw above timberline was gray rock and naked tundra. In an earlier century, when the village and its region subsisted on the food it grew, such a failure of winter moisture would have threatened famine. Now our worry was to keep our fields from dying, the prospect of which, although hardly dire, was still demoralizing. The small-scale agriculture practiced in the village fostered a parental feeling of responsibility toward the land, especially the irrigated land. We were responsible for tending it in a frequent, solitary, and therefore personal way. We had a duty to assure its health. But now our principal means for nourishing the land, our liquid medicine, was unobtainable. We were powerless, and having no power, we were idle.

Slowly the moisture-loving alfalfa, timothy, and orchard grass grew dormant and then withered. Week by week I called on Lalo, and we glumly speculated about how much of which species would survive. Lalo engaged in those conjectures more out of habit than interest. For him the fields had become a distant, increasingly foreign country that he was unlikely ever again to visit. He rarely went outside, even to sit on the porch. His oxygen bottle encumbered him, and the outdoor air was as dry as flame. He was more comfortable in the kitchen, where his humidifier ceaselessly hissed.

As the grip of the drought tightened, the acequia commissions in El Valle and its downstream neighbor Las Trampas invoked emergency procedures that had not been used in decades: El Valle would divert the river's flow for two days, then release it for Las Trampas to use for two days, then back again. This stretched the interval between irrigations for an ordinary parciente like me to more than a month, and even then the amount of water that trickled down the ditch was paltry. Only rain would reprieve us, and the summer rains, which in a good year arrive to dampen Fourth of July picnics, were still far off.

The land across the river, which Lalo and I shared, was another matter. The pasture we used together, plus the next one immediately upstream that was Lalo's alone, were watered by a minor ditch that started a short distance up the river from Lalo's fence. Only we used the ditch, and typically we used it without limit — and without the supervision of a governing board. In spite of the restrictions imposed on the acequia abajo, I continued guiltily irrigating both pastures, the upper one of which held a half dozen cows. Lalo had placed two horses in the pasture we shared, and I would have added a third to the group, but the land, even with clandestine irrigation, could not support two horses in so dry a year, let alone three. Rather than bring my own horse from winter pasture back to the farm, I reluctantly sent Smokey off to earn his living as a cow pony in the care of Tim Stasel on the Rowe Mesa grass bank.

Unfortunately, I could not keep the fact of my irrigation secret. Where water met soil, the grass turned green, and although the pasture's few green islands lay across the river, and the river was screened by cottonwoods and distant from road and houses, they fairly shouted their presence through the valley. They made a splash of brightness in the valley's tableau of drought. Even an eye less guilty than mine, glancing from a car or pickup window half a mile away, would note the flicker of foreign green through the windblown trees and pause to take a longer look. My neighbor Clarence Mascareñas, Lalo's brother-in-law and a commissioner of the association that supervised all the ditches in the valley, took me aside and somberly told me to desist. He explained that what we called the *acequia del otro lado* — the ditch of the other side — was entitled to water only when the main ditches of El Valle and Las Trampas were full. He delivered the edict gently, and he mentioned that the fines could run to quite a lot of money. The next day I closed the headgate of the little ditch, and as the following days grew into weeks and the relentless sun bore down, I watched the otro lado's tentative green islands fade into the surrounding brown, the horses gnawing all the while.

Every field suffered, the pasture supporting the horses worst of all. Parts of it were soon as bare as a dirt corral. But Lalo had nowhere else to put the horses. With Clarence's help he'd already sold nearly all his cows, and his dried-out pastures could barely support those that remained. And selling Babe, his bay mare, was out of the question. Lalo was a horseman; he would sell his last cow and all his land before he would part with his saddle horse. Nor could he return the black gelding he was obliged to keep for someone else. Giving up Babe would have been tantamount to surrender, and in his condition surrender of any kind seemed mortally dangerous. I resolved not to trouble him about the horses or the pasture, and instead when I visited I brought him news of other things, all of which, one way or another, were connected to the drought. Ranchers were screaming about stock reductions on the parched national forests, and as the politicians and the so-called experts from the ag college down south joined in, the general level of delusion and incoherence was becoming fairly entertaining. Meanwhile a forest fire had raged past Truchas, a village ten miles away, forcing road closures and evacuations, and it might have threatened El Valle except for a lucky change of wind. And there was news of other fires—the whole Southwest seemed to be bursting into flame—including a holocaust in Arizona where two very large fires merged into a single giant one that consumed a half million acres of ponderosa pine and filled our sky with smoke for weeks. The smoke was so bad that Lalo hardly dared to stick his head out the door, even in the cool of night, and he listened, patient and amused, as I told him how the smudged sky had turned the moon into a baleful orange disk that glared through the night clouds like an angry eye.

Our visits took place in the moist enclosure of his kitchen or in a tiny, adjacent sitting room, where there was a daybed, a single chair, and an old television with a snowy picture. The hiss of the oxygen machine, which he now used day and night, joined the ceaseless hum of the humidifier. The vinyl tubes that tethered him to the tank were like a long mustache, which he absently patted and smoothed. His world had shrunk to those two rooms, his bedroom, and a bathroom. Since he couldn't go to the porch, he scarcely looked out the windows. The stories I told him seemed to strike him as distant and unreal, like programs on television. He would ask about Babe, and I could always tell him she was fine. I would ask about him, and he would say he was doing okay. The treatments weren't too bad, he said, and when the rains came and the air wasn't so hot and dry and full of smoke, we would sit together on the porch and maybe he would come down to the river and have a look at things.

A dry field feels like concrete underfoot. The grasses stab before they break, and they do not bend. In the first stage of dryness, the natural green of the grass melts away and a reddish brown replaces it, and in the second, the red wears out, as though abraded by the sun. In the end, only a yellowy brown remains, a color like urine, so thin and tired the land seems naked, nearly skinless, with the suffering organs of the soil all but visible.

The spirit of the land wanes too. The ceremony of first water had failed. The ritual conversations with Lalo, assessing weather, animals, and crops, had changed in character. They were one-sided and increasingly abstract, as though their content no longer mattered. Worst of all, the season of growth had come, but nothing was growing. With nothing to irrigate, I took to wandering more than usual. My wife and children were consumed with activities in the city, and the business of the village and our farm receded in their minds. It was an easy temptation to haunt the desiccated fields, brooding too much, taking my regrets for a walk and mourning the beleaguerment of the land, my friend who had died, and my friend who was dying.

But the land never speaks in just one voice. Even as the burnt fields mirrored and amplified the spirit of things gone wrong, little havens of comfort and moistness remained, tucked away in a grove of trees or hidden in the nook of a canyon wall, and each recalled a memory. Under a certain stand of cottonwoods where the soft spring-fed ground threatens to suck off your boots, I had once helped Lalo's father gather calves. We cornered two against a screen of trees, and Jacobo handed me the lasso. "I am too old. Throw it," he said.

I must have looked as bewildered as the calves. "I don't know how," I pleaded.

"Throw it anyway."

So I threw it and the noose settled around the necks of both calves together, and I yanked it tight. The calves tried to bolt in opposite directions, neutralized each other, and froze. They stared at me, astonished. I stared back with the same wide eyes. The old man laughed until he had to grab a tree to keep from falling down.

Up near the head of the acequia del otro lado, the ditch rounds a bend where its wall is leaky and thin. After a flood of spring runoff breached the ditch and eroded the bank beneath, Lalo, our neighbor Alex, and I spent a long day wrestling fresh-cut cottonwood logs into the blowout and shoring up the bank. We crowned the bulwark with a line of sandbags, all the while with Lalo giving directions and whistling "Árbol de la esperanza," loud and happy and shrill.

The weathered gray bridge that Alex and I built from scavenged lumber is shaded by the tallest trees. It spans the river a yard above the surface of the water, but in 1998 yet another flood — this one a flash flood from a summer storm — tore the bridge from its moorings. Having lost bridges to other floods, I'd tethered this one to a tree with an ample length of chain, and when the flood picked it up, it swung with the current and eddied against the bank. In its hour of violence, the river built a sandbar for the bridge to settle on, and when Alex and I went down to survey the damage, there it lay. I built a new pier of juniper trunks to anchor it to an eroded bank, and then together in two days of heavy labor Alex and I winched it back in place and were exultant.

Under the blast of the sun, the land seemed stripped bare, shorn of identity like a head-shaved prisoner. But in the shade of riverside trees or the cool darkness of night, its old character came out again, and it became cluttered with remembered tasks and encounters, games with children, conversations with friends. I read somewhere the description of an opera house that became as vivid for me as though I had been there. The interior of the hallowed theater, it was said, gleamed golden and colorful with all manner of plaster cherubs and guidons and interwoven wreaths. But the lavish ornamentation accounted for only part of the aura. A special feeling resided there because the walls of the vast room wore a patina of heartache and desire. They had been gilded not so much with paint as with the longing, fear, and joy of the characters who had sung out their hearts on its stage. It was as though the walls had been lacquered with layer after layer of sublime and exquisite emotion, which the most beautiful music in the world had wrung from the air like a kind of dew. When you touched the burnished railing of the balcony, you touched a glaze of passion.

Familiar land can be like that. Wind and weather scrub it of melodrama, but it brings past to present in the same way. Actual lives and events, played out in a place, leave their traces in a kind of leaf fall of memory that settles, year by year, on everything. As I prowl the farm, I feel the leaf fall of my own time in an almost physical sense, and I imagine it falling on the mulch of generations gone before. I kick with my boot and scuff open the litter where it is thick, revealing a musty black mold, and think, that's from the days of Lalo's childhood when he herded goats through these hills. Scuff again, and there's the stratum when Jacobo was a boy and stoves and skillets were luxuries. One more kick and I touch the days of Mexican independence, and below that, the building of the old mill. Now the soil is thin and yellowing as I kick into the time of the Comanche wars and the settlement of Las Trampas. A few millimeters more, and then comes the substrate of unrecorded time when people from a long succession of tribes wandered through the valley, sizing it up, hunting and using what they could, and then wandering on to the next valley, only to return and leave again, these many different groups of people, some who passed their genes to the Pueblos of today, some who left behind no trace in flesh or name. I imagine the steady decay of the mulch of their experience, which before it disappeared yielded a humus of place and culture that fertilized the life that came after.

A friend of mine, a scientist, lost his teenage son to a freak accident, and only days later, with sorrow etched in every line of his face, he eulogized his child in a high school gym packed with classmates, friends, and family. I remember that he seemed the most composed of all the people there, and in precise, clear terms he presented an analysis of death. Things die, he said, so that creation can continue. And their death is not just a matter of making room. For creation, not simply replication, to continue, newness must continually arise. Which means randomness must be a condition of life. And so some things just happen, and some effects have no particular cause. In certain instances, random change might produce a flower of surpassing beauty, genetic resistance to disease, or a fortuitous meeting. But randomness, being morally neutral, just as easily sends a sledding boy into a steel pylon, or brings on the devastation of drought or the riotous growth of tumors. These things make a whole, he said, and render inseparable the twins of pain and beauty, loss and re-creation.

Randomness also generates uncertainty, not just the uncertainty of not knowing what to do, but the uncertainty that arises from not being able to predict, beyond the inevitability of death, how anything will turn out. The loss of a son would ramify onward in incalculable ways. There was hardly any point in imagining them. In the same way, Lalo's illness would go on, and so would the drought, and there was no knowing how long either would last or how great the damage and other consequences would finally be.

As it turned out, the drought outlasted Lalo. He enjoyed a brief reprieve in August, when a few scattered rains gentled the weather. He took to sitting on his porch again, and one day he elatedly drove down to the river in his truck, as he had pledged to do. But the disease soon seized him more sternly than ever, and from there his decline was inexorable. By November he rarely left his bed, and in his room you could almost taste the opiate haze and feel the ebb of his life. We buried him a few days short of Christmas. And in El Valle to say "we buried him" is not a euphemism to describe the work that strangers are hired to do. A backhoe sent from Las Trampas had dug the hole, and after interment, it was up to Lalo's relatives and neighbors to fill it up. I fetched a shovel from my truck and other men brought shovels from theirs, and, taking off our coats and draping them on gravestones or handing them to the women to hold, we shoveled several tons of dirt onto the casket of our friend.

The winter that followed was unremarkable in its outward aspects but indelible for me. It was the winter of the final disintegration of my marriage, a winter of scant snow, short days, and long nights, a winter, coming on the heels of drought, that seemed to amplify the drought's spirit of contraction and decline. It was a winter of fierce solitude, through which I walked my walk, circling the familiar hill, time after time.

It was a winter through which the Romero house, which had sheltered generations of the family, remained dark, night after night. I had never seen it like that; in fact, no one then living in the village had ever seen the house so dark and cold, all winter long. It stood like a sentry post beside the road, at the start of the village where houses first begin to cluster. Now the post was unlit, the garrulous sentry gone, and the whole valley, in a way, unguarded.

There were changes in the land as well. Lalo would have been intrigued by the slow death of piñon trees on the slopes behind his house. It was a gradual phenomenon, as the trees faded from green to rusty brown and dropped their needles, victims of the drought. Clusters of piñones behind my house died too. The drought did not kill them directly, so much as weaken and leave them vulnerable to the masses of bark beetles that surged in population on the bounty of ailing trees. By the time a new irrigation season arrived, a black acne of dead and naked pines splotched the hills on the north side of the valley.

That spring the mountain snowmelt was hardly abundant, but it was enough to bring the river up and fill the ditches. Once again water coursed through the arteries of the valley. It glimmered in the evening ministry of first water, and in time it licked the hard-caked portions of the hayfield that the drought had scourged. Most of the field greened up, though portions showed more bare soil than grass and took the better part of the summer to return to life. As the weather warmed and one turn at irrigation followed another, it was plain to see that the general productivity of the field was much reduced. The grasses and alfalfa showed little aboveground growth, presumably because they were replacing roots that had withered in the drought, or at least I hoped so. The story was different, however, in the pasture on the far side of the river, the land that Lalo and I had tended together. Except for surreptitious elk, which filtered down from the hills on dark nights, no animals grazed it that spring.

The last of Lalo's cattle had been sold, and Babe now had the run of the pasture, immediately upstream, that they had vacated. The young black gelding that had quartered with her the previous summer was one fence away, separate and lonely, in a field that abutted the two pastures at the river. My own horse, Smokey, had died that spring in a sorry and unnecessary accident on the grass bank, just weeks before I would have brought him back to El Valle, and I hadn't the spirit to get another. The result was that the otro lado was empty, and so its grasses grew ungrazed and unchecked.

It remained empty for nearly the entire growing season, far longer than I had seen it or allowed it to be empty before. And all the while I irrigated it as though its growth and fecundity were vital to the world. Had Lalo been alive, he would have laughed and told me I was loco and insisted I rent it to someone for cattle. I might have muttered that the pasture needed to recover from the year before when the horses had eaten it to the ground, but in truth its recovery was so strong that it did not need to rest for as long or as completely as I was resting it. With no horse to support, I had no immediate need of it, but I could not decide what else to do. I did not want to look at someone else's cows, and I was curious to see how the pasture would fare if it were not used. But the main reason for my inaction was that my personal world was in such disorder that nearly any decision seemed a heavy one. Down in town, I was camped out in a temporary apartment, my son barely speaking to me, my daughter heartbroken, my work a hurricane of demands, and the negotiations attendant to divorce becoming a marathon of guilt, anger, and sorrow. In the small matter of the pasture, I wanted to avoid choices; I wanted to coast.

And so the irrigated grasses grew from a ragged lawn to a deep veld by mid-July. They rustled and rippled in the wind. I had always assumed that Kentucky bluegrass was their main constituent because of the thickness of the sod and the durability of the best ground under heavy use from cattle and horses. Until this year, much of the field had resembled a rustic golf green, cropped down to carpet height and nearly as tightly woven. But now it was growing into something else.

Not that the land had never rested. From the late eighties onward Lalo and I had kept livestock off the pasture for the first months of the growing season. Our purpose was to establish a new generation of cottonwoods along the river, which we needed to protect the riverbanks from floods. Trouble was, the narrowleaf cottonwoods that grow along the Río de las Trampas reproduce by sending up new sprouts from their roots, and in May and most of June, from a cow's point of view, those sprouts are like candy. By July, however, the sprouts turn woody and hard, and the cattle ignore them if they have something else to eat.

But even the luxury of delaying grazing until July did not give time enough for the irrigated grasses of the otro lado to show what they could do. Now I was finding out. As July deepened and the soil grew hot, the grasses shot up at a feverish rate, even in the areas the horses had pounded the summer before. The pasture looked lush, Edenic. It occurred to me that perhaps the otro lado, in all its years of use, had never before rested for so long without being plowed or grazed. The settlers who first cleared and irrigated those acres two centuries ago probably plowed its flattest parts and sowed it to wheat or another hardy grain. They would have enclosed it within the single log and brush fence that protected all the fields of the village and into which livestock were admitted only after harvest was complete. But after barbed wire came along, fields that were too stony or wet or hard of access for plowing were fenced off as individual pastures. At some point the otro lado had been so reserved, with the result that cattle, sheep, goats, or horses would have barbered it every growing season thereafter with famished regularity. Under such hard use, the grasses must have reproduced through stealth. In nearly thirty years of watching, I'd never seen the grasses in the central part of the meadow produce seed. I was not even sure what kinds of grasses they were.

Soon the irrigated forage passed knee-high, and kept going.

Some of the grass began to produce dense, dowel-like flower clusters that confirmed it to be timothy, a mainstay of hayfields throughout the valley. Flower stalks shot up to the height of my waist and formed prodigious seed heads six inches long that swayed in the gentlest breeze. The other main constituent of the field turned out not to be bluegrass. It kept pace with the leggy timothy, growing slender and strong, and began to produce feathery florescences of a delicate color between lilac and rust.

This grass proved to be redtop, a species that was new to me. It grew so thick with the timothy that you walked through it with special care because you could not see your feet, and you did not walk so much as wade, shuffling your feet and using your knees to push back the grasses. As you made your way, you left a trail in the form of a shadowy trough, which the grasses, slowly unbending and stirred by the wind, gradually reclaimed. The sea of redtop and timothy engulfed the long strip of irrigated ground between the otro lado ditch and the cottonwood shade of the river. It was deeper and thicker than the hayfield crop that we were almost ready to cut. It seemed a vision of opulence, and as the redtop matured it imparted to the pasture a reddish cast, as though the field had been brushed with wine.

But the vision was incomplete. Years earlier, when Lalo was healthy, I used to find him sitting alone in the pasture on a fallen, solitary juniper, his shovel across his knees.

"Hola, Lalo. ¿Qué pasa?"

"Nada. Mirando las vacas, no más."

He was watching his cows. He liked to sit and watch them eat. He liked to listen to their loud chewing and see the mothers lick the white faces of the calves with their coarse, pink tongues. He relished the sight of the calves as they nosed in and poked at the milk sack. Their urgent sucking, when they settled on an udder, amused him. In watching his cows, Lalo was not just being dutiful. Of course, as a farmer, he needed to know how his animals were doing—if the big ones were healthy and the calves were nursing, and if all of them were accounted for—but this kind of watching was more than that. It was his pleasure, not just in the cattle but in the land. The cattle made the land animate; they gave it a story; they made it worth watching for long restful periods. They enriched its meaning. An empty field is like a single photograph: what is there is there, and when you have seen it you are ready to look away. But if you add cattle, you have added movement and change and a kind of animating animal heat—in cold weather you can even see the heat rising in shimmers from the red backs of the beasts. The cattle interact; they grow and change; they have individual lives: this heifer was born in an April snowstorm. She nearly died, but look at her now—she has a calf of her own. For an observer as keen as Lalo, those stories add up and intertwine; they stretch over generations of animals, and so the pasture, which to an outsider appears merely to be a pretty place with some creatures in it, becomes for him a place where characters, themes, and plots play out. It becomes a theater.

Cattle are not to everyone's taste, but for Lalo, who watched them carefully all his life and whose eye was keen to their minutest variations and peculiarities, they were far more entertaining than, say, watching men in helmets run into each other on TV or watching fat women talk about their weight. Cattle were real, and their stories mattered. The same was true of horses, and of the sheep and goats of the old days. Wildlife were real too, and sometimes conspicuous, like the fence-breaking elk that grazed our fields in the half-light of dawn or dusk, or the bighorn ram with the three-quarter curl that wandered down from the peaks two years ago. But wildlife are elusive and temporary, and their stories are not closely joined to the everyday stories of farming life and families in houses. It was cattle that mattered to a man like Lalo. Cattle and horses. He could watch them a long time.

And I had to admit, I could watch them too, horses especially. Their size, their graceful, long-legged form, their quirky marriage of brains and stupidity, wildness and docility, everything about them exerted its own magnetic pull. My field needed horses. I needed horses.

The otro lado also posed a second problem. The higher its grass grew, the more its opulence became a source of embarrassment. By the ethic of the village, such productive land wanted life and use. And I was not alone in admiring its wealth of grass. Tomás Montoya, whose farm lay upstream of Lalo's, let it be known that he would like to turn his two dozen cows into the pasture. Tomás was a friend of many years, but I demurred. Cows would trample out the beauty of the field in a day or two, and so many as he wanted to pasture there would leave a heavy mark on the regaderas and the fences. Besides, compared to horses, cattle were clumsy, shit-stained, and dull. Next year would be soon enough to bring them on, if I had to. But if I turned Tomás down, I had better have an alternative.

A co-worker and riding companion, Jerry Elson, was about to leave the state for several weeks. He had a pair of geldings who could stand to trade their dusty Santa Fe corral for the green feed and freedom of a mountain pasture. The change would do them good, and if I rode them once in a while, that would do me good. And they would animate the landscape with their sleek lines and equine alertness.

Years earlier Jerry and I, with a third friend, had spent a week riding from Santa Fe to El Valle through the mountains of the Pecos Wilderness. It took us four or five days. I borrowed Babe from Lalo for the occasion — I used her a lot in those years, when she was young. She had a flat, tightly collected dogtrot that was as easy to sit as a walk, and she could keep that gait all day long. She was a nearly ideal trail horse because she liked to cover ground and see what was around the bend. She was a problem with other horses, though. As Lalo put it, "She thinks she owns everything." And she required that her ownership be respected. There was another mare in our string on that trip, a heavy-set palomino, which Babe eyed with venom from the start. One evening I knotted Babe's picket rope too loose, and it slipped. The three of us were comfortably settled in camp eating supper when the scream of a horse pierced the air and we heard the sound of a heavy blow, like a baseball bat hitting a mattress. When we got to the horses, the palomino was backed up to the end of her line, holding a hind foot gingerly off the ground. Babe glowered at her with red eyes. She had kicked the palomino in the flat of the haunch and left the imprint of her horseshoe like a brand. The mare was only bruised and cowed, which was no doubt Babe's intention. If Babe had wanted to break her leg, she probably would have.

Now Babe would be in the pasture next to Jerry's horses, but as he was bringing geldings, not mares, I figured she ought not make much trouble. At least I hoped not.

It was August by the time Jerry brought his horses to the farm. One was a frowsy, pink-lipped gray that had faded to white. His name was Rowdy, and he was anything but. Rowdy had come on the ride from Santa Fe as a packhorse, and he had proved amiable, compliant, and stolid, commendable traits for a beast of burden. As a saddle horse, Rowdy was less noteworthy. He would go where asked, but he would not go there quicker than he could help it and the going would not be smooth. His trot was so loose-jointed he seemed in danger of falling apart, and his lope felt like he was trying the gait for the first time and didn't like it. In any kind of fast action, Rowdy seemed no more than half a step away from heart failure.

Rowdy's partner was TJ, a strong tall bay who acted younger than he was. TJ was the replacement for the horse that had carried Jerry on the long ride from Santa Fe. But where the other horse was athletic, the gangly, long-boned TJ was prone to trip. And where the other horse, even in new surroundings, quickly understood the lay of the land, TJ seemed perpetually lost. He was eager and enthusiastic, if he could decide what to be enthusiastic about, but things turned out badly when he tried to think for himself.

We unloaded the horses from the trailer on a clear afternoon and led them across the hayfield. We took off their halters at the gate to the river and watched them trot down the slope into the shade of the cottonwoods, where long stems of orchard grass angled against their legs. They stood and looked at the river. They looked at the trees and then at the grass with their ears pricked and their tails hissing through the air because of the flies. They looked back at us to make sure we weren't following, and then they dropped their heads and began to eat, ripping the fresh blades that grew closest to the ground and pulping the green mass in a slow audible rhythm: *schrush schrush schrush*. Then they sleepwalked a heavy half step forward, side by side, almost in unison. They snuffled the ground's sweet buggy salad and filled their mouths anew.

Jerry and I waited to see if the horses would cross the river and discover the feast of redtop and timothy on the other side. But they did not lift their heads. They shuffled half step by half step through the trees, swishing their tails and twitching flies from their backs. They sighed heavily and kept eating. The feast they had was feast enough.

The next morning, alone, I rise early and set out to check on the horses. The long shadow of the ridge still divides the hayfield into light and dark. The grass is heavy with dew, and the bird chorus brims with the prattle of robins and the buzz of wrens. A woodpecker hammers a hollow branch, and his drumroll echoes against the hills. A flycatcher whistles a question. The grasses and alfalfa of the hayfield are still uncut, and soon my rubber boots wear a wet paste of grass seeds and scraps of leaves.

Below the gate where we turned the horses loose, trails of trampled grass wind among the trees, but the horses are not there. I cross at the gray bridge and retrieve a shovel from behind a double-trunked cottonwood. Maybe I will move the water while I am in the otro lado.

A quick slosh across the irrigation water that has pooled under the tall trees, then a few steps up a bank and past a screen of young cottonwoods, and I am standing in the open sun. The blush of redtop stretches down the run of the wavy field. The horses are still not in sight, but two parallel troughs weave through the lake of grass. I wade into the damp green mass, which flags at my legs, and head for the unirrigated ground above the acequia, where the vegetation thins and the going is easier. No water but rain has touched the ground there, but even so the ungrazed plants have rioted with florets and blossoms. They've produced seed heads, fruits, and pods of all kinds.

Now I can see the horses in a curve of pasture, past a peninsula of graceful cottonwoods. Their trails end where they stand: they have not finished their first pass through the field. I approach along the upper edge of the ditch and stop when I think they might detect me. I lean on the shovel. The horses are head-down in the grass, which is to say their heads and necks have disappeared. So have their legs. All that can be seen are their burly irregular barrels floating on a sea of grass, their tails flicking, rippling the surface. They shuffle forward, and on this silent morning I can hear the muffled sound of their eating over the hundred yards that separate us. They move together as though they were one being, white shoulder next to red shoulder, white flank and red flank. If they had hands, they would be holding them.

A wall of trees rises behind the horses. The pale cottonwood trunks branch and arc with the light of the low sun spilling through them, and their backlit crowns fan up from the ground as though each were part of an eruption, each trunk tracing a different thrusting up and out, a different yearning for sky and space. From somewhere in the trees a bird I don't recognize shrills a two-note call. It sounds like "Who's there? Who's there?" The horses have still not heard or seen me. Heads down, they stalk slowly forward, tearing and crunching. Their backs swell with muscle. Their hides quiver. They raise their heads, scan the banquet before them, and plunge anew into the sea of food. Suddenly, close at hand, I realize I am a step short of destroying a prodigious spider web strung between a clump of broomstraw and a stem of wild rose. Dew glistens on the strands of concentric silk, and the maker of this marvel, a bulbous, red-legged, speckled-back creature, waits in the shadow of a rose leaf. The web is as big around as a washbasin, and the number of closely spaced strands within it seems infinite. All around is a profusion of plants such as I have never seen before on this unirrigated site: purslane, blue grama, western wheat grass, yarrow, an oat grass I don't recognize, mullein, lambsquarters, sweetclover, an errant alfalfa, sleepy grass, a seedling of wild plum, sunflower, and more.

Then the bird calls again, "Who's there?" The call is familiar, but I cannot place it. And the horses raise their heads, look left and right, and step forward. And the bird calls again. The horses plunge their heads, and in the near silence I hear them eat. Then the bird calls. And the horses raise and step. The moment repeats itself, another concentric strand. And again the call, the step, the look around. The return to eating. This is it, I think. Paradise, or something near it.

Everything fits; everything seems right. It is an hour past dawn in the moist field under a generous sun. The vigor and health of August infuse the land. The red beast and the white beast are content. And they step forward, and the bird calls, and they eat.

Suddenly a scream pierces the stillness. The horses jerk up their heads. We hear the drumming of hooves, but from where? Over there: a horse appears far down Lalo's field, running this way fast. It is Babe, who has scented the new arrivals. She's coming up through the adjacent pasture in big S-turns, galloping with her tail erect, ears laid back, lips bared in a snarl of white teeth. She skids to a halt at the fence and screams again. Her barn spike of sound stabs the valley. A translation requires no skill: "I'm a bitch!" she screams. "You're mine!"

A little sorrel I've never seen before has run up behind her. He's agitated and skitters sideways. She kicks at his face. He dodges and retreats beyond her reach.

Rowdy and TJ highstep quickly to the fence, Rowdy in front. Babe cranes to him. They touch noses; then she bares her teeth, screams, and wheels. The other horses wheel too. I hear bodies collide. A kick thuds. Fence wire screeches. A post cracks loudly, but the barrier holds. A cloud of dust, like one smoky chug from a locomotive, rises above the fray. The sorrel lunges at Rowdy over the fence and tries to bite him on the neck. Rowdy moves his head an inch out of range and disdains even looking at the sorrel. The dust settles. Rowdy's tail twitches a fresh hello to Babe, who steps anew to the fence and cranes at him again. They widen their nostrils and blow on each other, each inhaling the other's exhalation, making an exchange of breath, like an exchange of hugs or handshakes. Then TJ moves forward and tries to shoulder Rowdy away from the fence and the mare. Rowdy doesn't want to be saved by his buddy and stands his ground. Then a new sound of hooves pounding. At the fence, all four pairs of horse ears swivel toward the river. It is the black gelding in the pasture that lies catercorner to the mare's. He runs to the corner of his fence and looks longingly at her. She trots a dozen yards in his direction and glares at him. With a toss of her head she pivots, throws a kick in the black's direction, and then lays her ears back and dashes at the little sorrel, who's been tagging at her heels. The sorrel sprints away, tail tucked, puffs of dust rising from its hooves. Rowdy, meanwhile, has taken a turn away from the fence and is circling back to get another lungful of mare, and the mare heads for the point on the fence where they will meet. TJ tries again to shoulder Rowdy away, but Rowdy leans back into him and stays on course, so they stagger forward tilted into each other like a pair of drunken sailors.

Finally, for a moment, stasis is achieved: Babe stands parallel to the fence so that Rowdy can access the air space over her withers. Rowdy thrusts his head to the favored spot and sucks down gallons of her odor. As though to tell the other horses this adoration isn't important, Babe half closes her eyes and pretends to drowse. TJ, a half body behind Rowdy, is shifting his weight, eyeing his besotted partner. The sorrel, meanwhile, has crept back into the scene and stretches his nose to within inches of the mare's rump. And the black gelding at the corner fence despondently looks on, a score of yards away but completely out of reach.

A raft of clouds, strange for an August morning, has crept up out of the west and now hangs over us. Even stranger, a fat raindrop suddenly plops into the dust at my feet. And then another pings on the blade of the shovel. And one on my hand.

One on my hat. And now the fat drops are drumming all around, making the shrubs dance and the grasses shimmy. The rain sparkles in the sunlight, which floods beneath the clouds. The backs of the horses begin to shine. They stand immobile at the fence, massive and so warm-bodied that wisps of cool steam begin to rise from their withers. Babe and Rowdy are stolid, the others restless. I think of their breathing, deep and slow, filling the damp of their lungs, and I think of their ceaseless gut rumble and of the fountains of blood pumping through them. I think what an odd convergence of psychology and mechanics they represent: the ever-growing hoof that burns with the reek of hair; the fragile steel of the legs and their bowstring ligaments; the powerful muscles of the rump, like coiled springs, and the still more powerful shoulders and brute chest; the tough, danderous hide that encases it all; the tail that for sheer extravagance and luxury puts the tail of every other grazing animal to shame; and the elegant curve of the long neck, draped with long dark feminine locks of mane, and then the head so alternately cantankerous and noble, with its tender muzzle and almost prehensile nostrils, the teeth ever-growing like the hooves, the swiveling and expressive ears, the soulful eyes, which harbor in their brine weird growths that look like polyps on a deep sea reef; and then the brain behind the eyes, and whatever spirit or genie goes with the brain, which in their sum result in horses being as various and endearing and infuriating as people, which means that finding the right horse can be nearly as difficult as finding a partner with whom to share a life.

The rain patters down, warm and gentle. Undeterred by the wet, the "Who's there?" bird calls again from the cottonwoods. The horses seem to drowse, except for TJ, who remembers his stomach and fills his mouth with grass. He chews; the others merely stand. Then Babe's tail begins to flick. One, two, three times, and stays erect. A shudder runs through her, and she feints as though to rear and instead swells with air and spasms out a caterwaul that shatters the peace of the valley. She kicks at the sorrel, pivots, and kicks at Rowdy. Hooves flash, and mud flies. Bodies thud. Fence wires screech, and the melee starts anew. Dust rises in spite of the rain, and I think, no, not the tranquil beauty of mere moments ago. Instead this, the perfection of disorder and desire. The paradise of how it has to be. This is it.

Acknowledgments

The writing of this book began one spring morning at the Guadalupe Canyon Ranch in far southwest New Mexico. The first sentence of the first essay came to mind, complete and entire, and I wrote it down. A year and three-quarters later, the last major overhaul of the third essay, essentially the completion of the book, took place in the "Mexican bunkhouse" at the same ranch. I am deeply indebted to Drum Hadley and Rebecca West for their hospitality on both occasions, and many others besides.

Also vital was a stay at the Mesa Refuge in Point Reyes Station, California, in June 2005. My thanks to Peter Barnes for making such a retreat possible and for the good company of fellow writers Melissa Scanlan and Hilary Kaplan while I was there.

My biggest regret about this book is that I did not finish it before Max Steele, my friend and mentor for almost four decades, passed away in August 2005. My regret is a double one—that he never saw the completed work and that late portions of the book did not benefit from his critique. Much of the good herein is owed to him. Other readers whom I thank for their guidance and encouragement include Frances Kennedy, Dan Flores, Dinah Bear, Darla Sather, Tom Wolf, Don Lamm, Fred Altenhaus, Betsy Rogers, and especially Beth Hadas and Talitha Arnold. Barbara Ras applied her sharp editorial eye to the final draft and, deftly assisted by Sarah Nawrocki, guided the book to publication. Deborah Reade drew the wonderful map. Craig Allen, Tom Swetnam, and the late Fred Swetnam educated me about peeled trees. Jerry Elson and Crockett Dumas loaned several of the horses that run through these pages. Tomás and Fred Montoya and Clarence Mascareñas are present in these pages, even when not named, as friends and neighbors. And Lalo Romero, who embodied everything meant by the phrase *buen vecino*, is sorely missed. I am grateful to all of them.

Alex Harris and Margaret Sartor also read drafts of these essays, but my thanks to them goes far beyond their encouragement and helpful criticism. We are partners together in the land we own in El Valle, where the events described in these essays took place and where most of the book was written. Which leads to a confession: at times I present the farm as though it were all mine, without describing the tangle of our shared ownerships and occupancy. From a stylistic point of view, I could not repeatedly qualify statements about my relationship to "my" land without diminishing the intensity of the narrative. Moreover, the Harrises are present at the farm, where our houses are distant from each other, only for a month or so each summer, and the events herein described took place almost entirely in their absence. The long partnership with Alex, going back to 1972, and then also with Margaret and their children, Will and Eliza, has been one of the great joys of abiding in this place, and for all of that I give thanks and dedicate this book to them.